#Convict

Conversation
Criminal Justice Reform, the Corona Virus and America's Conscience

B.A., Charles Irving Ellis

Please visit: www.charlesirvingellis.com for comment and upcoming events.

Cadmus Publishing
www.cadmuspublishing.com

DEDICATION

This book is dedicated to the struggle, and all those treated unjustly.

Acknowledgements

I would like to thank my family for their love and support. To my teachers, mentors, and freedom fighters, the journey to change often starts with turning a page.

WAKE UP CALL

On January 19th, 2020 I was awoken by the sound of metal crashing against metal. I pulled back my blanket and blocked my eyes from the bright light that rained on my face. The cell I was housed in had a steel sink and toilet, a stand-up shower and a metal desk bolted to the wall. I stood up from my bunk and noticed nothing out of order. The banging was coming from outside the cell. When I reached the cell door, I peered out the glass window to see what all the commotion was over. I saw a uniformed officer pushing a food cart down the hallway with trays stacked on top of trays. When he reached the gate, he shouted; "I don't give a damn if none of you bastards eat."

"The milk is spoiled!" one inmate responded.

Then the tier exploded with another round of screams and door kicks. Not unusual action coming from the special housing unit, where I was housed at the time. But this incident was about more than a improper breakfast meal. It was the "kickback" from a long dirty list of mistreatments, forced upon the inmate population at Lompoc California, United States Penitentiary.

An outbreak caused by the mumps (yeah, the mumps), recently stopped normal operation and all inmates were confined to their units. Meanwhile, Lompoc officials allowed inmates from other facilities to transfer into the building, which subsequently increased the spread of the disease. To make matters worse, staff then decided to strip the inmate population of radios and proper hygiene products, to further cut us off from the civilized world and decrease our ability to properly wash our own bodies. And when frustration among the incarcerated reached a new high, staff members forced inmates to "cell-up" with other angry prisoners. To say the least, the environment inside Lompoc was made dangerous for all involved. Even still, you would think something so conducive to the orderly running of a prison, such as serving up-dated milk would be a simple task. And you would be wrong. Welcome to my reality.

A science study revealed that, your average American spends over 35 years of a normal life span asleep. Asleep, meaning unconscious or none responsive. If true, that is half a lifetime, with our eyes closed. No wonder justice moves so slow! It's not that we can't feel the effects from a tarnished system that victimizes more lives than it protects. And it's not like we don't care. Rather, when the blindfold is finally lifted from our symbol of justice's old eyes, it often takes her a good while to lift her lids, put down those heavy scales and get that plated ass on the go.

As a prisoner, I have served over fifteen years inside the Federal system, and never felt more compelled to speak out against the many cruel issues that are destroying lives, and creating a cycle of abuse both inside and outside our society more than now.

According to a 2008 study, more than one in every 100 adults in America are in jail or prison. Between 1972 and 2008 the adult population in the American penal system soared nearly 600% from 330,000 to 2.3 million, 20 years ago, states spent above 11 billion on corrections annually, and today it is about 52 billion. 68% of prisoners meet the criteria for substance abuse or dependence, 60% do not have a high school diploma or general equivalency diploma, 30% were unemployed in the month before arrest, 55% are estimated to have serious mental health problems, 14% were homeless at some point during the year before they were incarcerated, and we are not even scratching the surface that keeps real issues that disable the incarcerated buried.

There are conversations being held over Justice Reform and the effects of mass incarceration. But how can we seek change without first speaking with those that are directly impacted by decisions being made behind closed doors? How can you truly help someone you do not know, without attempting to first understand them in the least? You can't!

There are conversations being held, but the lives of those in which make up the heart of the conversations are not being truly considered. We are not even invited to the meeting. As an adult, I feel offended that those who claim to work for my benefit never took a second to inquire what might actually help me. Therefore, your actions belie your words. But that's alright. There will be many who will say: "You're an inmate, you don't know what's best for yourself." And there lies the real problem. Which is, if you can only see me as an inmate, who needs to be controlled at all times, what then is the difference from being incarcerated and being "free"? Furthermore, if I do not matter while in here, then surely, I do not matter out there. Titles such as "inmate" do not define a man, no more than a designer shirt changes one's character. Incarcerated or not, if you see me as nothing, then nothing will change. I write this, not to abash, but with clear intentions on provoking change. Our justice system is broken, and unfortunately, I live in this shattered home. What I have experienced would, and should shock the brain. I only hope that any jolts you may feel will motivate you to speak out, rather than turn a clenched eye. In this system, we (prisoners) are not allowed to be human. My often times belligerent assertiveness gets me into trouble, but it was civil rights activist John Lewis who best described what "Good trouble" should be, and the cost of engagement:

"I came to the conclusion that this may be the price that I have to pay to a people and our movement to move this nation closer to a society based on a justice that values the dignity and the worth of every human being. We had to do what we could to redeem the soul of America."

-Rep John Lewis

This is a man who marched with King. Who will march for us today? The first step is to garner attention. If no one knows your struggles exist, how can you succeed?

Not with standing, the "First Step Act" was passed into law, allowing the Government to create new programs that will help return offenders to society sooner. F.I.R.S.T. S.T.E.P: Formerly Incarcerated Reenter Society Transformed Safety Transitioning Every Person. The bill dictates that people sent to federal prison, "must" not be placed further than 500 driving miles from their homes. It bans the shackling of pregnant women, and also offers increased "good time credits". This is a minor victory. Or is it? The bill was passed into law in 2018, and after four federal transfers, I remain over 2,000 miles away from my family, as prison officials continue to manipulate the first step act in order to cheat inmates out of relief. The baneful stares and twisted facial expressions alone cause me to believe that, the "bone" thrown was not without objections. Prison employees have become so accustom to viewing the incarcerated as less than human, I imagine they find it hard to suddenly forget their training; and like disgruntled zoo keepers, they are being forced to release those they have long considered animals.

I understand that words alone may not be strong enough to change the minds of many. But to the correctional officer invested in inmate bashing and systematic bullying, I ask: Are you the hero or the villain? Or would you rather be an extra in this film, watching each event unfold without uttering a single line in dispute of the cruel and unfair treatment of others? Is it your job to help, or are you only motivated by self-corrupting goals, such as job security and social acceptance? *We will get back to you on that.*

Meanwhile, there are laws in place that allow every criminal prosecution in our country to be carried out unfairly. Prison guards hold professional titles, while committing crimes against the men and women they are hired to protect. Drug users, all over the country are coddled while drug dealers are pummeled with serious time for the same offense. Mental Health continues to go unchecked (or over looked) as cell mates clash and criminal influence is free to infect others. Family ties are systematically destroyed. A deadly virus spreads throughout the country while prison staff members neglect their directives and operate with complete indifference. Men become boys, convicts become inmates and individuals are forced to join the horde in a psychological war aimed to emasculate, dehumanize and erase self-esteem from the incarcerated. How can we move forward? Let's talk about it.

I was placed in the special housing unit (solitary confinement) at Lompoc U.S.P, for an alleged introduction charge. After being interviewed by a member of the prison staff, it was clear to me that I was being accused of something I did not do. But the Administration refused to drop these allegations. Instead, they placed other prisoners in solitary confinement in order to force confessions out of anyone who would substantiate their claims against me, I asked the head authority figure in the building (the warden) about my constitutional rights, and he reminded me: "As an inmate, you are only intitled to the rights we provide you."

I wasn't allowed to receive mail, newspapers, magazines or books. After four months of this treatment, the Administrations doubled down on their unlawful tactics. They no longer allowed me: soap, deodorant, toothpaste or lotion. In December 2019, I went before a hearing officer to answer for the juggled charges jammed together and was told that I had no right to see the evidence against me. The alleged narcotics were said to have arrived through the institution's mail system, and when I demanded to see photo copies of the envelope in question, I was told that I could not examine staff member's claims. The hearing officer found me guilty without cause, or pause and suspended all visiting rights for a year. He then took my phone and commissary privileges for six months along with over three months of good time credit, and charged me a money fine. Seeing that I had already spent over 100 days in solitary confinement, he was kind enough to only sentence me to 60 more days in the hole.

The appeal process was blocked at every corner, as superior officers refused to correct mis-conduct by their co-workers. I wasn't allowed to see the sun for over ten months. My personal property was shuffled through, then jammed into boxes as they prepared to transfer me to the ADX complex at Florence Colorado. I lost communication with my loved ones, as my support system began to weaken. I was completely cut off from the outside world and oblivious to world events. As I prepared a new wave of complaints and grievances, I realized the damage had already soaked in. More importantly, who would listen to a prisoner?

Those who refused to help the Administration were tortured and shipped a few thousand miles away from their home addresses (despite the first step act). The abuse of power was evident, mixed with a complete lack of concern for prisoner safety. Lompoc, in my opinion, was an ideal location for the spread of infections, of all kinds.

I could hear the whispers in the hallway as I was being escorted to the transportation unit. My stomach searched for a decent meal. My facial hair was unkept and dry. My skin looked life-less, but I could feel there was something in the air. A secret no-one wanted to share. No one wore a mask, *not yet*. But their mouths were sealed as their eyes spoke volumes. I wanted to ask a few questions. My silent concerns were growing louder. But to them, I was just an inmate who didn't deserve an answer, even if it would help my own safety.

"As an inmate, you are only entitled to the rights we provide you."

An hour later the ocean passed on my right side. I could smell the pacific. Handcuffs cut into my wrists as the transport van pushed forward. The three-hour drive brought us beyond the gates of Victorville U.S.P.

"Welcome to Victimville!" A over hyped guard announced as I maneuvered my leg irons past him, and into the building.

A lot of Federal prisoners have fears of California prisons, and rightfully so. VictimVille was not a nice place, but it wasn't my first visit. It had been years since I walked the cold hallways, but I still recall the obituaries posted on bulletin boards, crooked officers looking to make their bones (or break a few), staff suicides and inmate riots. I could still smell the bloodstained floors from armed disputes that often lead to criminal indictments and FBI investigations. Victorville wasn't a nice place at all.

I went through "in-take" thinking about all the corruption that lives in a system that claims to protect and reform. At least that is what the government tells the American public. But somewhere between the fake cell room photos they post on their websites and the mis-leading program statements, the true point of "corrections" is completely lost. I have learned through personal experience; reform is not even a part of the real agenda. Not even a little bit.

After all the chains were removed, I was brought to the "holdover unit" on the east side of Victorville, where prisoners are held until the U.S. Marshals arrive with new transportation orders. There was a T.V. in the center of the unit. I stopped to get a look at the screen, and my eyes widened at the headline: *Former basketball star Kobe Bryant was killed in a helicopter crash along with his daughter and seven others.*

My sorrow never had the chance to speak. The next head line blind-sided me. I felt a pain in my chest, the result from sudden worry. It rose up from my stomach and pushed against my heart. News line after news line reported a virus sweeping across the country. I thought about my family. Were they safe? Was anyone I knew sick or infected? I hadn't heard from my loved ones in half a year due to the unfair treatment at Lompoc. Panic started to build up, it quickly turned into anger. The phone system was shut down for the night. *I wouldn't be able to use it anyways.* I searched my surroundings for answers, but in the end, I was forced to take my emotional combinations to an unfamiliar cell with dim lights and cold walls.

The next day, the Administration informed the prison population that we would be on "lockdown" status. All transportation would be cancelled until further notice. Updates would be provided by the FBOP. News headlines continued to pour in: U.S. prisons and jails on alert for the spread of Coronavirus.

Covid-19 (as it was called) was reported to have no active cases in the Federal Bureau of Prisons on that date, then the number of infected jumped to 115 prisoners, and 89 correctional employees. It was hitting America hard! I learned that Lompoc had over 35 confirmed cases of the virus only weeks after I was transferred. I was desperate to contact my family and confirm their safety but my phone use was still suspended. I began to think about the abuse I suffered at Lompoc and realized how I narrowly escaped serious exposure to a deadly virus. Then I thought about those who didn't. And in a system that considers hand sanitizer to be contraband, I began to ponder on how much time I had until the virus reaches us all.

I write, not to appear holy or altruistic, but in hopes that my words will not be disregarded. Many of us pray to a higher power, or meditate for strength to go on, without actual proof of success, because often times hope is enough. Although I am a prisoner, my soul remains free. So if you are willing, I will do my best to show you where I am coming from. But this ain't no chicken noodle soup for the prisoner's soul, it's more like an ice-cold iron for the devil's ass.

Harsh reality: Prison is not a nice place to live. However, the bureau of prisons wishes to manipulate the American public into believing our prisoners are being treated fairly, while silently violating human rights and disregarding the same policies they have written themselves. Prison officials operate with enmity. Constitutional rights are circumvented. A punishment- no reward credo has been adopted throughout the system as the Administration invents new ways to provoke the prisoner. Meanwhile, inmates commit social suicide in search of values that only help to destroy them. Pace, if there is going to be change, that change must come from within. We cannot continue to expect justice, compassion and fairness from those programed to deny us these exact things. Equally so, we cannot allow others to speak on behalf of us, in a silent war that imprisons our liberties without making every attempt to join in, even from a far.

Therefore, I give you a true account of events that have shaped my opinion and ultimate judgement of our justice system as a whole. I.E, those that are hired to secure, protect and reform the convicted have long delt in a physical and psychological system of abuse, in order to destroy the prisoner (but keep them breathing) by inflicting punishment that will have long lasting effects, far after the term of imprisonment. Whether you agree or disagree, I appreciate your mind. Albeit, we should first allow the facts to have the floor. So, before you judge a book by its cover, I ask for the conversation to be had.

PREAMBLE

We the people of the United States, in order to form a more perfect union, establish justice, ensure domestic tranquility, provide for the common defense, promote the general welfare, and secure the blessings of Liberty to ourselves and our posterity, do ordain and establish this conversation for the United States of Americas convicted.

TABLE OF CONTENTS

CHAPTER 1

GUARDS

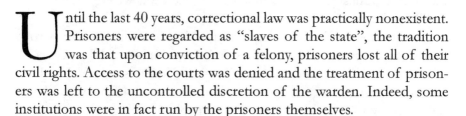

Until the last 40 years, correctional law was practically nonexistent. Prisoners were regarded as "slaves of the state", the tradition was that upon conviction of a felony, prisoners lost all of their civil rights. Access to the courts was denied and the treatment of prisoners was left to the uncontrolled discretion of the warden. Indeed, some institutions were in fact run by the prisoners themselves.

Until the 1960's, the courts had adopted a "hands off" attitude towards prisons. This is no longer true. It is widely accepted that prisoners retain all of their constitutional rights upon entering the prison system that are not necessarily withdrawn by virtue of prison security, discipline, and necessity. In short, a prisoner takes the constitution into prison with him.

Litigation over the past 40 years has shown that not every denial of a "right" involves a deprivation of a "constitutional right". As a practical matter, courts, state or federal, do not wish to become involved in the administration of prisons. They only become involved when there is no other alternative. Given a reasonable alternative, courts will and do defer to the administrative process. This doctrine was mandated by the PLRA, where prisoners, in general, must exhaust all available administrative remedies before filing federal lawsuits against prison officials.

A good friend of mine once applied for a job as a correctional officer. She had designs on becoming a state trooper but fell below requirements on the physical exam. Her desire to serve and protect lead her to the federal bureau of prisons, where a lawful adult who meets all requirements can find stable employment. Right? Not exactly. Although the FBOP struggles to maintain a full staff at most facilities, they continue to turn away a special type of societies own. Thus, my friend returned home from her interview in tears. When I asked for the cause of her unguarded emotions, she explained:

"They are all savages!"

"Well, some prisoners have mental issues", I answered.

"Not the inmates, the staff!"

"What happened?"

"They won't hire me because my point of view when it comes to the inmates doesn't match their own."

"What do you mean?", I asked.

"They put me through a series of questioning and scenarios, and when I answered honestly, they continued to tell me I was wrong", she said.

"What kind of questions?"

"Is the inmate a human being? I said yes but they said that's the wrong way of thinking. I sat there confused for almost an hour while they scolded me on the right attitude to have. They said inmates are scum and will attempt to manipulate me. But it was him who was manipulating. I know right from wrong, and I'm more then capable of doing my job without becoming corrupted. But it was him trying to corrupt me at the door. He said inmates need to be treated a certain way, never trusted and constantly punished. People make mistakes. Isn't being in prison the punishment for their crimes? I don't understand, what is the point in belittling them or treating them less than human. I just don't understand."

But I understand all too well, and the shortage of willing employees is no coincidence. It's the effect from faulty criminology and the attempts at brainwashing rational thinkers.

"Reason and logic often have no place in prison"

-Shon Hopewell

In the early eighties, federal correctional guards were trained to be professionals; from their attire, down to their interaction with the prison population. Their approach was respectful and none confrontational. The administrations motto: Firm but fair. A guard's actions were carried out with accountability. Guards wore shirts and ties, and performed their duties with minimum aggression towards the convicted. The federal system at that time, was designed to confine the convicted as they served their debt to society. The prison guard was ordered to keep prisoners confined and safe. However, somewhere along the time line, in-between the so-called war on drugs and mass incarceration, it would seem that the mission statement of occupation in the FBOP has changed. And thus, a new title for our prison guards: Correctional Officers.

Today, the over whelming majority of correctional officers are ex-military personnel. They carry backpacks to work and dress in uniforms that resemble the armed service. Each "Officer" is required to wear a protective Kevlar vest, black boots and name tags. They are equipped with prison patches on each sleeve, along with a utility belt complete with radio, keys, flashlight, handcuffs and OC spray. These men and women report for duty strapped up. But it's the attitude they bring with them that often causes conflict in every institution around the country, ultimately doing more damage to the convicted then all the gadgets in their tool belts.

For over a decade and a half, I have watched the constant abuse of power, physical assaults and psychological smack downs on prisoners, at the hands of these so called "correctional officers". The guards of today are not trained to be firm and fair. They are programed to become bullies and "inmate bashers". I used the word "programed" specifically and intentionally. Like robots, correctional officers are not allowed to think for themselves. Their responses are preset. Any unfamiliar question or situation presented by the convicted are met with evasiveness (stand by) or suspicion ("let me pat you down"). Prisoners are thus, treated like foreigners in a camp, rather than citizen seeking rehabilitation.

In fact, correctional officers are dressed for combat and sent to work housing units with no actual directives, leaving the convicted unsure of the rules to be followed. Staff members are screened thoroughly through interviews before being allowed to work inside FBOP institutions. The overall views and acceptance of the incarcerated play a major role of the hiring process. New correctional officers are placed on probation periods at which time, they must demonstrate their indifference to the actual plight of the prisoner. Correctional officers are told how to think (Not at all), respond and act in every situation, when dealing with the prison population. Like robots.

There are many different levels of security in the FBOP. Each classification requires prisoners to be housed in different institutions. Prisoners are shipped to high security (USP), medium security (FCI), low security and federal camps, all over the country. And each level brings more and more abuse from correctional officers toward the prisoners. While serving time inside a high security, prisoners are often physically abused at a high level. Medium security allows increased mental and verbal abuse by its officers. Officers enjoy using a prisoner's "medium status" against him by threatening to increase it to a "high" if they do not accept the abuse inflicted. The verbal abuse reaches new heights when prisoners are placed inside low security buildings and camps. The administration justifies these action by convincing the prisoner that it is a privilege to be incarcerated at a less violent facility. However, being incarcerated is no privilege at all. And the administration has provided their own form of violence by way of verbal and mental abuse at all levels. No one should be abused, period! But what the administration has successfully achieved is, forcing the prisoner to choose lesser evils:

High security=physical abuse, medium security=mental/verbal abuse. How can the system continue to allow this and call it reform?

"If you want others to be happy, practice compassion. If you want to be happy, practice compassion."

-Warren Buffet

In true army fashion, correctional officers take orders handed down by their superiors, without question or hesitation, regardless of the possible violation to a prisoner's rights. I have heard correctional officers proudly state, "I spent years overseas fighting for my country. I have numerous confirmed kills. I'm a real soldier."

This type of chest thumping often happens in the dark hallways of penitentiaries, where high fives are exchanged while a prisoner is being physically assaulted or drug to solitary confinement. I don't believe these "officers" truly understand the gravity of their own words. I.E, if you are a "real soldier", that means you follow orders no matter the cost. There could be lives in jeopardy, but as long as the officers follow orders, even with a blind conscience, he will be honored by his superiors. But I find it hard to believe that "confirmed kills" make a man feel good about his service to our country. In fact, I strongly believe it causes a dilemma in the "right or wrong" process (unless you are a psychopath). And this alone should make one unfit to look after the well-being of others.

"To a hammer, every problem looks like a nail."

Many of today's correctional officers have deep seeded regrets, mixed with post-traumatic stress, common with ex-military type and brought to work with them each day. To a politician, this might seem like a perfect fit. American soldiers and American prisons. But the foundation of prisoner abuse, both physically and mentally start on this toxic pairing of unstable inmates and a staff mostly made up of ex-military men and women with mental illness, and combat trained brains. Correctional officer suicides continue to rise as facilities across the system shut down operations in order to hold memorial services for the deceased.

How can we expect prisoners to return to society reformed when prison guards are programmed to abuse them? But that's not the half of it. The inmate bullying causes frustration and anger to grow inside its target, but the "correctional officer" doesn't stop there. Its common practice for an officer to "shake-down" a prisoner's cell and leave his personal belongings in complete disarray. Officers conduct "pat searches" numerous times in a single day until the prisoner becomes cantankerous, then punishment is involved. As if serving time isn't enough, many correctional officers take it upon themselves to increase the sentence by degrading the prisoner. I have witnessed correctional officers push aggression towards an inmate then issue an incident report (write-up) when the inmate responds negatively.

C.O. (short for Correctional Officer) banter often involves illegal tactics that are used in order to make a prisoner's life much harder than the judge sentenced for. The sentence is the punishment, so then, what's up with the suppression of human rights, such as the right to be safe from abuse? The constitution is the supreme law of the land. Any laws, status, regulations or government policies in conflict with the constitution are unenforceable. This is the standard by which all government action is measured. The constitutional rights of prisoner's policy states: Every person, including an incarcerated felon, has the right to be free from the fear of offensive bodily contact. Yet and still, correctional officers continue to physically threaten the incarcerated. Policy states: It has generally been recognized that prison officials are privileged to use force against prisoners in five situations 1) self-defense, 2) defense of third persons,

3) enforcement of prison rules and regulations, 4) prevention of escape, and 5) prevention of crime.

Can you see how one policy negates the other? E.G., how can a prisoner be free from fear of offensive bodily contact and actual offensive bodily contact when prison officials are privileged to use force against prisoners to enforce prison rules and regulations? These policies are made up and manipulated to suit the writer. Prisoners are told they have no right to self-defense while incarcerated, but policy 3.3 "self-defense" states: Every person has the right to protect him or herself against an assault by another. So then, why the double-talk? Why does the FBOP continue to post wonderful photos of their many facilities on their website, when in fact, they are painting a false picture? I have lived in many of those locations and the truth is, prison reform is not in the best interest of our justice system. But you know what is, job security!

Prisoner abuse, misuse and manipulation is "business as usual". Men and women being released from prison need not be reformed or mentally sane for that matter. There are plenty of empty beds, and prisoners are still being forced to live with other prisoners. Safety is not a priority for the prisoner. Pace what prison officials might offer. Convenience is more important, but not convenient for the prisoner, oh no! The needs of staff are always placed first. (Hence the over lapping number of infected, staff vs. inmates throughout the Coronavirus crisis) "every inmate will be provided toilet paper, when it's convenient for the staff to pass out". Every inmate will receiver three meals a day", when it's convenient for staff to ready. All prisoners have constitutional rights that will not be violated or over looked. That is, unless staff feel you don't deserve those rights rewarded to you by the constitution of America. Prison guards pass out mail when they feel like it (if at all), make rounds when not too busy (research Epstein and Hernandez cases of suicide), and attend to the well-being of the prisoner "whenever they can". Officers take off running down the hallway when an alarm is triggered. To the naked mind, it seems as if they are in a pact to stop a physical dispute between prisoners. In reality, staff members are trained to respond with such urgency, not for the well-being of the prisoner, but firstly for their fellow staff member in the event that he or she might be in distress. We (prisoners) are serving time, but for all intense and purposes, we are on their (the Administration) time. That is why every memo concerning the inmate population always puts "staff safety" in front of our own. They decide what we should or should not receive.

"Prison is not a nice place to live."

Violent, aggressive, untrained and abusive officers arrive to work with clear intentions to punish the prisoner.

"That's our job", one officer claimed.

"They are convicted felons who broke the law and cost the American public more taxes", another justified.

"They deserve to be punished, and consistently."

"So what if the guards are bullying those guys. They are in jail."

"It's the correctional officer's duty to rough them up a little."

"It's all a-part of the punishment."

Right, I don't think so…

Furthermore, why is the correctional officer's well-being held above the prisoner's? do their lives mean more? Or is it because they are said to be law abiding, honorable and with out ill intentions? You might even nod your head in agreement with that last statement. But reality tells a different tale. That is, if our correctional officers are so much better than the crooked inmates they suppress, why then are CO's being "walked off" prison yards though out the FBOP system every month? Hmm…

Walked off: when a guard is found to have committed an illegal act on institution grounds or otherwise criminal activity.

Offenses range from bringing in illegal substances for prisoner use, carrying an unregistered weapon, or having an inappropriate relationship with an inmate. Illegal actions could lead to criminal prosecution, law suits or other penalties. And while the FBOP scrambles to keep these dispositions under wrap, the Administration continues to present the "correctional officer" as holier than thou. The truth is, we all make mistakes, bad calls and poor judgements. So then, why is the convicted treated less than human while those hired to look after our safety continue to commit crimes?

Correction officers are hired to protect the building, not the inmates. In fact, it would seem, they couldn't care less about the lives they are paid to look after. Unless of course, the cameras are working. The Administration has created many crafty ways to "appear" as if they care. Hence my favorite: When the incident alarm is activated, all staff members are told to give their best running attempt to reach the event, no matter their location at the time of the alert. On the contrary, when an inmate activates the duress button in his cell, the officers on duty take their time and when they finally arrive the attitude Is confrontational as if they were pulled away from their favorite show.

I have seen knife fights that went on for hours. I have witnessed guards beating prisoners while in handcuffs. I have heard inmates screaming in pain in the middle of the night, calling for help as staff members laughed. I have watched prisoners request not to be forced into a cell with another prisoner and subsequently murdered by his cellmate, because of staff apathy. Does this sound like the work of professionals? Where is the correction in the officers? Today's prison guard lacks problem resolution skills, confrontation de-escalation and the common compassion to promote reform. They inflict pain on the inmate to address any wrong. And this might be firm, but it damn sure ain't fair.

Not all correctional officers are bad. But the empathic are drowned in a "tough on crime" wave that forces them to turn away from speaking out in favor of job security and social acceptance. Thus, they are among the rest, stuck on dilemma like Effie Trinket from The Hunger Games, while carrying out their duties. Rather than push for a solution, they became accommodationist, providing medication for a curable disease.

The real problem is, the Federal Bureau of prisons has engaged in a silent psychological war against the prisoners they claim to protect. They call us "inmates" while referring to their own as "officers". American military personnel understand better than most, the influence of words on attitude and behavior. They call us inmates to destroy our self-esteem and lower our self-worth. If it's a "inmate" you are dealing with, then that makes it easier to accept the way they are being treated. But if it's a man or actual human being, the level of mistreatment becomes harder to accept.

At the same time, prison guards are handed lofty titles to enhance their value and self-image. Their safety and mental state are priorities, and their word is the Gospel when compared to inmates. Depending on the "Officers" superior, he or she is often above the law. But correctional officers are just taking orders, right! Like robots, right! Why so hard on them? You're right! Prison guards are only a small piece of the problem. They are programmed to follow orders without thought or objections. They are taught to value job security and social acceptance. Speaking out would only turn them into vagabonds or pariahs. So let us talk more about the men and women that control these androids. They are collectively call: The Administration.

Similar to the armed service, there is a chain-of-command, with Washington DC (The Government) at the top of the pyramid. When interested, they send down orders to the director of the FBOP. Below the director is the "Central Office". They receive the mandates and pass them down to the "Regional Offices" located around the country. Then it's the warden's job to brief his staff and carry out The Administration's wishes at all cost. The Administration stands behind their workers faithfully, impowering them to carry out the directives exactly as ordered from the programmer's mouth. *Well in theory.*

But there's a glitch in the system. Mandates are not carried out correctly. Wardens are allowed to free style the direction of their staff while reports of misconduct often never make it out the basement. If I recall, our government really doesn't want nothing to do with prison politics. They reluctantly agreed to take a look at issues, only when or if said issue makes it pass the defensive line of "Administrative Remedies". Believe me, this is a hard goal to tackle. It's like throwing a football to a receiver, who happens to be covered by nine defenders, and hoping not to get intercepted. Prisons quickly becomes communist societies as wardens decide to practice totalitarianism on our hidden citizens. Prisoners are directed to write a grievance and send complaints to the same office that passed down the order in question. In my opinion, this is like complaining to the restaurant manager about a waiter's actions, when those same actions were ordered to be carried out by the manager. In short, they're on the same team. The administrative remedy process has become a game of pin-the-tale-on-the-donkey as prisoners complaints travel building to building with indifference stamped on the front page. There are some remedies rewarded through the filing of proper paper work. But they are by far the exceptions, and do not alter the fact that correctional officers carry out cruel tactics ordered by superiors and over looked at the top of the pyramid. So, what do we do?

"We can't allow the inmates to run the asylum."

Of course not! Especially seeing that the abusive priests are doing such a wonderful job.

With remedies exhausted, I look to the people. And to the correctional officers torn between right and wrong, side lined by the submissiveness in the face of misjustice. Who will you be? Courage is the strength to face uncertainty while infected with fear. How long will you stand next to a co-worker who incites physical altercations with prisoners then takes measures to see prisoners suffer for a very human response? How many inmates must commit suicide after clearly displaying mental issues and only receiving a face full of gas (spray) brought on by a team of bullies wearing enough armor to storm a castle? Can we solve conflict in less violent ways? Or will you continue to hold your tongue in the interest of job security? If so, then you are cowards, and unfit to save lives both socially and physically.

In Andre Norman's book, "The Ambassador or Hope", he speaks about compassion for the incarcerated. This is a man, who after serving time, decided to reach back into the forgotten and provide sound programs to help others rehabilitate, using language they could relate to. This is someone who actually cares about the outcome, and that's what it takes to promote positive change. Because if you don't care, neither will anyone else.

The Coronavirus had infected over 2,800 federal prisoners, 300 staff members and killed over 50 inmates. The news report claimed. The lack of due diligence played a huge part within the prison system. I should know, I'm in it. And as the numbers grew, "officers" increased joshing: "we have to protect the weak!"

Meanwhile, the Administration did not hesitate to use force against frightened inmates. Guards neglected to us a mask. Social distancing became a tool to punish the population of prisoners. Such as, a full lockdown labeled "Quarantine" with over 100 inmates who not only never contracted the deadly virus, but never showed any symptoms of being infected. But I'm getting ahead of myself (don't worry we will get there). In fear of being called "soft on crime", the FBOP often ignores a prisoner's legitimate health concern, while working to protect themselves from outside scrutiny.

As a consequence, there are men and women returning home from prison worse off, both physically and mentally. They are full of anger and resentment over years of mental abuse and dismissive treatment. "We must use fire against fire." I once heard a Lieutenant brag. But using fire only creates a blaze that will spread and hurt none violent offenders. The threat of physically violence by correctional officers is at an all-time high. This inmate bashing and systematic bullying must stop. Only then can we evaluate what will truly help.

Our correctional officers are armed with combat boots, vest and high-powered propelling weapons. Yet, the administration continues to seek out extra protection for officer's well-being. While the prisoner is handed a "bed roll" and threatened with further punishments for attempts to protect himself from future dangers. Prisons are not nice places to live. I agree! But today's prisons are made dangerous by the men and women that work in them. Mental illnesses run rampant. And instead of providing proper mental health assistance, guards are ordered to deal with the mentally distraught with physical force. Either that or give him a cell mate, which creates new problems. These tactics have not worked, don't work and will not work. Question! If the prison population is so violently dangerous, that officers have to arrive at work locked and loaded, ready for war, then why is there no concern for the prisoners being forced to live among each other? Are our lives not important enough to take precautions? We will come back to that.

In closing, whether you call them prison guards or correctional officers, the professionalism continues to be missing throughout the FBOP. It has been replaced with infringement and indignation for the incarcerated. The Administration sends down rules to suppress the inmate, with no concern over the effects such action inflict. The Administrative remedy process is a bad joke, just another tool to keep the hamster on the wheel. Long before any relief is granted, the damage is already complete, and prisoners have given up on a system that claims to protect their rights. Most recently, a new warden will arrive at an institution and completely destroy normalcy among the prisoners by taking earned privileges for no clear reason, then he leaves months later to take a job somewhere else. This strategy leaves the inmate confused, and wondering what he could have done to deserve such treatment. And by the time a prisoner's complaint reaches the appropriate level, the warden who disrupted the compound is enjoying his retirement. It's very effective. It forces the prisoner to work over time, trying to regain niceties he never deserved to lose.

These tactics are designed to antagonize the inmate population. It's a win-win for the powers that be. If the prisoners act out violently, more will be taken and the previous acts will seem justified. If we respond peacefully, no action will come of it, and we will learn to live with less than we earned.

These mind games leave lasting impressions on the prisoner, and mental bruises of inadequacy. Subsequently, we are taught to never assume good conduct will bring rewards. Also, to never trust a system claiming to be firm and fair. Like prisoners of the 40's, it would seem that we are guinea pigs, being used to test new ways of controlling a population both physically and mentally. The Administration needs to be reminded that prisoners are still human beings, American citizens, fathers and brothers, sons and workers.

The next step should be to re-train the correctional officers. Prisoners need positive reformation of thought through courses that work. You cannot help correct a violent offender's actions by offering him violence. That would be the same as treating a drug addict by prescribing more drugs. "Stay Woke!" The narrative is lost when you use the same method you are warning others against. Prison staff members must learn how to use compassion. Problem resolution skills teach others how to use positive actions to defeat negative thinking. The Administration method of "take! Take! Take!" creates a cycle of confusion, and kills motivation completely. How can the convicted learn that, the right actions will bear fruit, when every action, not matter right or wrong is met with punishment? They can't!

Thus, ex-offenders arrive home mis-guided, frustrated and uncertain of their own thoughts. We cannot teach others respect for the Law, by committing lawless acts. Simply said, hurt people, hurt people. And without a true understanding of the facts, we are ultimately hurting ourselves. Let's see what the Constitution says about these terrorist tactics on the incarcerated:

The history of the present Administration is a history if repeated injuring and usurpations, all having in-direct abject the establishment of an absolute Tyranny over these prisoners. To prove this, let facts be submitted to a candid world.

Abusive actions, both physically and mentally
Depredation of personal property and human rights
Verbal abuse and unjust fines
Suppression of independent thought
Forced associations and physical conflict
Lack of protection and proper mental care
Cruel and unusual punishment
Abuse of power
Unfair treatment and Biased performance
Induced self-inflictions

Bullying and inmate bashing

Physical assaults

Dehumanizing conditions

Lack of compassion

Mis-direction and interference in the pursuit of happiness

Social assassinations and the division of family ties

Tampering with mail

Third party extortion

In every stage of these oppressions, we have petitioned for redress in the most-humble terms: Our repeated petitions have been answered only by repeated injury. An Administration whose character is thus marked by every act which may define a tyrant, is unfit to be the keeper of a people...

Wow! And that's the Constitution. Well, most of it. Let's talk!

CHAPTER 2

SNITCHES

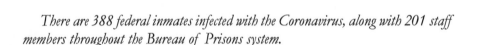

There are 388 federal inmates infected with the Coronavirus, along with 201 staff members throughout the Bureau of Prisons system.

I listened to the morning news as reports continued to pile up. The covid-19 was moving fast. Every day brought higher numbers of the infected. I was surrounded by worried prisoners and indifferent guards. The president issued a stay-at-home order to promote social distancing in an effort to stop the spread, and slow the outbreak. I returned to my cell after a brief shower and wondered if the guards were being tested properly before arriving to work. There was a chilling silence in the building. I watched each officer working our unit very carefully. It was still unclear what level of safety would be provided to protect the prison population from infection.

I couldn't help but to remember how I first arrived in California. It was the second week of December, 2013. I was escorted by two guards from a small van, and onto a landing strip in Pennsylvania. My handcuffs were connected to a chain locked around my waist. The cold steel cut into my wrists as the armed guards nudged me forward. Another officer asked me to open my mouth, stick out my tongue and rotate my head side to side. When he stepped away, I shuffled my feet along the cold concrete. My shoes were more like paper gloves, made to clean up dust around a gym floor. It was already difficult to walk, the shackles clamped around my ankles didn't make it any easier.

My jumpsuit seemed to be made out of tissue. It allowed the chilly morning air to pierce my skin. I felt a sting of pain in my foot. I looked to my right and noticed transportation vehicles parked along, and around the air field. Men and women wearing outfits that resembled my own were lined up, all in chains and visibly shivering, in front of busses and unmarked cars. I thought about the slave ships that traveled to this continent some five hundred years ago. Then despair grabbed my face. My steps began to slow. My rebellious soul kicked in, but my intelligence offered it reason. I was headed on this journey whether I liked it or not.

Unlike the bodies brought over in bondage, an airplane was my captor's choice of transport. As I made my passive approach, my eyes landed on the old commercial carrier in front of me. I saw a group of officers holding high powered assault weapons, and circling the area. There was a large amount of tape wrapped around one of the plane's wings and my fear of flying found new heights. I quickly looked to the guard on my left. His pale face showed no sign of compassion. I stopped at the bottom of the ladder, and looked up the long staircase and shook my head. Then I noticed a smiley face imprinted on the front of my cloth-like slippers. *These people got jokes.*

But there wasn't nothing funny about being transported by the U.S. Marshals. They are all work, no play. One false step could land you in the back of the plane with a bag over your head. My concerns didn't matter a bit. There would be no first-class treatment or balanced meals on this flight. The mission: Protect the plane and its "Cargo". In that order. And as a Federal prisoner, I have learned that the United States is very sufficient at keeping the chains on, both physically and mentally.

The FBOP is known for randomly removing prisoners from one facility, and placing them inside another that needs warm bodies to fill cold bed bunks. Thus, human beings are shipped all over the country in chains. Men and women are transferred thousands of miles away from their families with no warning or cause. I walked down that narrow isle looking left and right at the sad faces of confinement already strapped in their seats. A U.S. Marshal pointed to his left, then I spun my body into an empty chair. It wasn't my first time on "CONAIR". I had no expectations to experience anything new, but this particular flight was a little different.

There was an old white man seated next to me, I didn't pay the inmate much attention at first. We exchanged a head nod (the universal, but silent "what's up"), then my eyes searched the plane for familiar faces. Once every seat was full, and all restraints confirmed, I leaned my head back and prepared for the lift off.

"Where you from?"

I heard a rough voice in my ear. I turned my head and found the old man starring right at me. As the plane entered the clouds my stomach tightened. I scratched my nose, cleared my throat and said, "I'm from Boston".

"Boston! That's my town," the old man's eyes lit up.

I twisted my lip to the side in disbelief and looked him over. He was wearing the same blue paper suit each prisoner rocked, coming from MDC Brooklyn. He appeared to be in his late seventies, and didn't look anything like the Mayor of Beantown.

"These pricks have changed everything", he noticed my look. "I hear guys calling screws C.O. and it makes my blood boil. Correctional Officer is a professional term. There's nothing professional about these pricks. Last time I was in the system, we called them guards," his low growl lingered on.

"So, this ain't your first rodeo?" I asked, more amused then concerned.

Then his old face crumbled up. It created more wrinkles then a balled-up paper bag. "I served my first trip on the Rock. Things were a lot different then.

"You did time on Alcatraz? That must have been a minute ago." I had read about the first Federal super max and the prisoners who attempted to escape through the dangerous ocean. "Did you know Alvin Corpes", I asked.

"We called him Ray", he spoke out the side of his mouth.

I sensed his willingness to talk, and my interest grew. "So, what they get you on this time?"

"These pricks are playing politics; they knew where I was the whole time."

I noticed his aggression. He had the demeanor of a man who enjoyed a long history on the other side of the law. He didn't seem to be some white-collar crime offender, or a corporate hedge fund swindler, taking a dive over mis-managed funds. He had a tough exterior, one only a life on the streets could forge. He wasn't someone's friendly grandfather taking a federal vacation over a crate of moonshine either. No, I began to recognize him from the news reports and his subsequent trial. He wasn't just some old geezer. He was a gangster.

"What you say your name is?" I played dumb.

He slowly turned his head towards me, raised his chin and gave a half grin. "My friends call me Jimmy."

I nodded my head in return. I didn't know where he was headed, but I had read a good deal about where he had been. I was sitting next to American's most wanted. I thought, what were the odds of two guys from Boston Massachusetts being seated next to each other, on a flight to confinement. It was a three-hour ride to Oklahoma. And I heard he liked to talk. So, I relaxed my head and gave him both ears.

"They claim I was on the run for sixteen years, but that's all bullshit. I had immunity! How could you be looking for me, when I'm flying in and out the country on your airlines? I took trips to Ireland and back. I visited all the sights, me and my gal. The Alamo, the Grand Canyon, you name it. These crooks are liars and they stole my money. They just wanted to make a big show out of me," he huffed.

"They say you are a rat", I said with a straight face.

"That's just bullshit. The game was played differently back then. Everyone was trying to get the goods on each other. It was leverage! Cops, crooks, thugs, thieves, it was all the same. They loaded me up with LSD, then sent me home. I was winning! That was the real problem."

I could see the veins in his neck jumping, as he tried to explain his ignominy. "I thought you said you had immunity".

" I did! And those crooked sons-a-bitches knew it too. That's why they snatched me up. Everybody is in the dirt. They figured I couldn't lean on the facts no more. But their all in on the take," he said.

I shook my head, but remained silent. A few seconds later, he started up again.

"First chance I got, I shouted I'm guilty! But they wanted to make a show out of me. I was in isolation, under a camera. They used armed motor cades to bring me to court and forced me to wear a Kevlar vest.

All for show! Then they refused to allow me to plead guilty, stole my money and paid millions for my defense. All for show."

I continued to allow him to ramble on without offering any rebuttal. I would occasionally say, "that's crazy." Or interject a, "for real!" But just to keep him going. Ultimately, I found it entertaining that a notorious government informant continued to make excuses for his actions. A reprobate.

"They knew where I was the whole time." He repeated, more to himself then to me. "I ran my building. Everyone came to me for advice. I'm no rat! I played the game how it's played. Now look, we are inmates instead of convicts, and they are C.O.'s instead of guards. That's bullshit! Everything has changed."

Our plane rolled into Oklahoma's terminal as the Marshals readied their belongings. The old man beside me scoffed at the Marshals walking the aisle and turned his nose up at the other prisoners looking in his direction. Like he was a stand-up guy. Then a voice called out: "Listen up for your name! Step forward and recite your number. James Bulgar!"

Every head on shoulders turned in my direction, I saw the look of excitement on many faces, as they tried to get a good look at the guy seated next to me. When he rose to his feet, I pushed back in my chair to let him pass.

"Here we go." He grumbled and stepped in the aisle.

I heard whispers raise while the man known as "Whitey" made his way to the front of the plane. No one spit on him or threw tomatoes. There was awe in some prisoner's eyes. After all, this was the guy Hollywood chose to make several movies about, while glorifying his activities and protecting his legacy. But there was one thing, not even the industry could soften. He was a snitch! And nothing else mattered to those that still stood up to shake a man's hand. Once you are labeled a rat, a snitch, everything else about you is a footnote, and not worth mentioning. Sure, you played the game. But you cheated! And there is no Hall of Fame for cheaters. Is there?

After lending my ears to the Boston Banger, there was one thing that lifted an eyebrow. It wasn't his lavish living, or the secret dealings with the government. Old whitey had a point. Things have changed, and we have watched while our Justice system deals dishonorably, manipulate minds and twist laws. There are many who may not see the snitch as the

"Thief of Justice" or seed of corruption, but allow me to explain why you are wrong.

The earliest recorded record of the snitch is in Manchester, Vermont in 1819. Soon after, the snitch became a formal part of law enforcement. During prohibition, the ATF used entrapment as well as informants, making "snitching" an integral part of the justice system. In the 1970's the use of the snitch exploded during Nixon-Reagan, and the so-called war on drugs. Today, 60% of drug defendants cooperate in some way with authorities in exchange for reduced charges or sentences. The Government barters with offenders for: cash, drugs, a chance to spare friends or family from criminal charges, reduced sentences and charges dropped in exchange for information on others. These quid pro quos have successfully made snitches the leading cause of wrongful convictions in our country. Good Samaritans? No! A snitch is out to gain at all costs, true or false, and prosecutors are their enablers. Not convinced? Let's talk about it.

When I was nineteen years old, I received a scholarship to play basketball at a small college in West Virginia. Shortly after arriving, I realized I could purchase firearms at the local pawn shop. I did not have a felony record, drug abuse or mental illness. But there was one thing I lacked. A state I.D. so I asked an older woman, who was a resident of the state, to purchase the firearm on my behave. In my adolescent mind, I never thought these actions would change my life forever.

But as faith would have it, my college career was side lined due to a fight inside a fast-food restaurant, that left me facing serious charges. My attorney advised me that if convicted, I could no longer possess a firearm legally. Understanding the gravity of the situation, I decided to sell my hand guns before my trial date and predicted conviction.

After my trial, I was sentenced to State prison to serve three years. When I was released on parole, I had intentions on putting my life back together, if not for myself, then for my three-year-old daughter. But the ATF had other plans for my future. I was indicted on February 22nd 2006 for dealing in the business of firearms. The charges claimed, I bought and sold dozens of guns. In truth, I only purchased four my entire life. But the prosecutor wasn't interested in the facts. Only focused on gaining convictions, they pressured me with threats and serious time, in order to force me to help them incarcerate others. And when I refused,

I was convicted and sentenced to 27 years for a crime that holds a ten-year maximum term. Cold world!

But my true crime wasn't dealing in firearms. It was refusing to become a snitch. A snitch is a individual that helps law enforcement convict others on crimes they may or may not have committed, in exchange for escaping the penalties for crimes they have committed themselves." The government hired repeat felony offenders to take the stand, raise their hand and recite the script they were given. In exchange, the government agreed to turn a blind eye to criminal actions, past and present. A snitch doesn't care about, what he or she has to do or say in order to survive, or return to their life of lawlessness. Their only mission is self-gain. And our government has a lot to offer. I don't think you fully understand. A snitch is not a law-abiding citizen who witnessed a crime and has stepped forward to assist justice. No! A snitch is a criminal, who has been given an offer (By law enforcement) to escape punishment for his or her own crimes if willing to help convict another.

Now then, is this someone you want in your friendship circle? Can you imagine a snitch living next door to you, committing felony after felony and watching everyone else, so if ever caught, he will have enough leverage to get out of jail free of charges? Snitches have no moral code. They will help convict people they do not even know. Snitches are used in 90% of criminal cases. They receive gifts in the form of favors from prosecutors in exchange for their assistance. Who else but a lawless creep would lie under oath, help steal away another person's liberty and feel no responsibility for their actions? These actions may be beneficial for those with no sense of self value, and if you decide to live your life as a snitch that's your choice. But I have a choice also (or at least I should) not to associate with you.

The government threatened to give me 95 years in prison if I didn't help them convict someone I barely knew. They were willing to tell me what to say in front of a jury, and when I refused, they over punished me for having principals. I received 27 years because I refused to help convict another. That was my choice, and I stand on it.

We all make choices, and often have to live with the results. However, no one should be forced under penalty to accept, associate or otherwise befriend an unsavory character. It's dangerous, and unfair. Yet and still, our government continues to pay these individuals to take the stand, lie under oath and help manipulate evidence against others. These actions corrupt our country. It's a sweet deal for the snitch. Their moral compass was thrown out the window long before the government approached. And with a super power such as The United States backing their scandalous moves, I imagine they feel very comfortable. They don't care about the defendant's family or the lives they help destroy. They only care about themselves. They are felons with no reason to turn away from a life of crime. But it's not them who swore to protect the American Constitution (5th Amendment), now is it?

I do not want to be around a snitch, nor befriend one. I have a constitutional right to be safe in my surroundings. I have a right to protect myself from harm. That includes, never allowing a known or suspected informant into my personal space. I have heard law official say: "If you're not breaking the law, you don't have to worry about a snitch." But that's not true! Prosecutors possess the power to indict a garbage can. The way our justice system works, if the government wants you or someone you know, for a suspected crime, they will threaten to convict you as a tool to convict another. Your life doesn't matter. Your friends' lives don't matter. The snitches life doesn't matter. The only objective for our prosecutors are convictions. Point period.

The truth is, you are innocent until the prosecutor is convinced otherwise. Once this happens, he or she feels it is completely fine to break the law in order to bring you down. Look at it from this perspective: If I believe you committed a crime, I need not prove you did it. All I have to do is find someone (credible or not) willing to say you did it; and hopefully you will admit to it, or agree to give me someone that actually committed another crime. *Business as usual.* The essence of a snitch is the unlawful life he or she is committed to. It allows the government to use their own actions against them, and weapons against others. A lawful citizen lacks the diabolical mentality that snitches maintain. No motives, no pressure to lie. Consequently, with such a system in place, it can be argued that the truly dangerous are not in here (if so, not for long) but allowed to remain in society.

I expound this point, in hopes that you may begin to understand why a snitch (or rats as they are often called) is an undesirable person among the convicted. Their presence alone is a physical threat. Not because I am committing criminal acts, but for the fact that all they have to do is say I'm committing criminal acts, and with the backing of our justice system, I may very well be convicted, innocent or not. Now, would you want to live in a small space, the size of a broom closet, with a criminal who is prepared to do anything to satisfy him or herself? Why then, is it fair (or maybe firm) to force prisoners to live among those that put others in danger for selfish gains? Prison is not a nice place to live. Personal property, family information and identities are left unguarded and exposed while the "thief of justice" lurks freely.

Most recently, staff members have attempted to change the narrative, by redefining what a "snitch" is, to fit their own agenda. These efforts amount to folly as far as intelligent minds are concerned. But for those that might fall victim to the shenanigans, let's talk about it.

"What happened?" I heard a guard ask his co-worker.

"I shook down cell 112, took some photos and the inmate snitched on me to the L.T."

"that's a rat!"

"Sure is." The guard replied.

On the contrary, no it's not! You and your family are out dining in a restaurant, and you find a piece of hair in your soup. You call for the manager and inform him about the particle in your food, then the waiter walks by and says," Stop snitching". Are you a rat? Hell to the no! No one was taken to jail or brought up on charges. As a human being, you have a right to fair treatment. Even as a prisoner, you expect to be treated with respect. It's a correctional officer's duty to perform their own policy, the proper response is to ask his superior to "pull em up", check his actions for better compliance. Prisoners cannot allow others to violate them or their personal property, then remain silent out of fear of being labeled a snitch by the same officials who lock them in for a living. That's how resentment builds and tension boils over. And then it explodes. Those same "officers" will line up to testify against you in a court of law. "He's a violent criminal".

Understand the games being played below the table. If the administration can successfully manipulate the meaning of words (like snitch), they can dupe us all into believing, rather accepting that it's no big deal, and everyone does it.

"Mom! Jimmy took my toy.", said little Billy.

Did little Billy just rat Jimmy out? Telling is telling, right! I didn't think so. But there are many who want us to believe what little Billy did was equal to "snitching". Why? Because snitching helps the government incarcerate whoever they want, for whatever reason, regardless of an actual crime or none at all. It's the ultimate weapon for the miscarriage of justice. Part of the correction officer's job is to seek out what a prisoner has done wrong with in the rules, write a report, send him to the "hole" and testify to what happened at a hearing, in writing or in person. They are giving a salary to report violations to their superiors, and when a prisoner reports them for rude or unnecessary actions, the officer now calls the prisoner a snitch. Things done really changed.

Now back to reality. A snitch is someone that reports a crime or otherwise "cooperates" for self-gain or favor with authorities. A snitch is not a law-abiding citizen who gives testimony to a crime they witnessed. A snitch is not someone complaining about the service of a worker in order to receive better treatment or what they deserve. And it's not poor little Billy hoping to get his toy back from his bullying big brother. *Fuck little Billy!*

No seriously, we tend to miss the signs when we don't pay close attention. The truth is, most people have opinions that are shaped by their personal experiences, and what has been done to them. So, when I say I don't want to associate with rats or snitches, I have good reason to not want to be around those who are ready and willing to say or do anything to benefit themselves. Informants are offered "get out of jail" free cards. They are not concerned whether their testimony is true or false. Their only concern is getting paid for their services. Prosecutors push: Say this and you go home. A week later, the rat bastard is on the streets beating on his child's mother, or robbing a bank. And why not? If caught, all the snitch has to do is play informant on someone else, and he will be home before Christmas. Are these the type of individuals you want in society? Men and women, committing crimes with immunity on their minds. It's a lawless game, and the value of life is extremely low.

So, what do we do? First, no convicted felon should be allowed to testify in a criminal case. Yes, I said no convicted felon. I can imagine every prosecuting attorney across the nation shaking their heads right now. But this is a rational remedy. A convicted felon is not allowed to vote in the overwhelming majority of the states in our country. A convicted felon cannot run for high office or own a liquor license. A convicted felon cannot receive special housing approval in our neighborhoods. A convicted felon cannot purchase a firearm. A convicted felon is so unsavory, employers steer away from hiring them, even when they are fully capable of performing the job. So then how can they be trusted, or relied upon to help take away the freedom of an American citizen? (And often their life sentenced to death) They can't!

If a convicted felon is not honorable enough to be allowed to take part in a criminal trial as a jury member, how can he or she continue to be allowed to take the stand and help sway the minds of those directed to find guilt or innocence? The answer is simple. But big business is not. Government officials will say: If convicted felons cannot testify in criminal trial, there will be crimes that go unpunished due to lack of evidence. (Kind of like the crimes you allowed to go unpunished in exchange for a snitch's assistance)

Not with standing, my response is this. If a convicted felon's word is the only evidence in a criminal trial, then the defendant should be acquitted by way of reasonable doubt. Is it not reasonable to doubt a convicted felon's word, who has been paid in one form or the other to provide said "evidence"? or, will we continue to allow unfair trials in the name of "Mass incarcerations"? Convicted felons taint every trial they appear in. Their presence alone should garner a mis-trial. Why? Because their motives are for self-gain. They are performing a job, not a duty. And no one's life, nor liberty should be taken from them after a trial infected with deceitful elements.

Today's law enforcement consists of special tactics and technology that helps to gather true evidence to present, and determine if a crime was committed, and by who. If a convicted felon is the only one who can tell us about a crime, with no other surrounding facts, his or her word is not enough. That's why convicted felons are often used to strengthen weak cases. They testify to facts given by prosecutors and law officials, who have decided that suspicion of a crime is enough, and conviction is the only goal. Prosecutors put convicted felons on the witness stand to lie, because often times, they are the only ones willing to do so.

The anti-criminal psyche forces us to focus only on the fact that a crime was committed. Someone has to be held responsible, and brought to justice. However, if a defendant is to be convicted beyond a reasonable doubt, and a convicted felon is the soul evidence against him, based on our country's lack of faith in all convicted felons, that evidence is never enough. A convicted felon should not be allowed to testify in a criminal case. There are thousands of American citizens serving outrageous prison terms, based on the testimony of a convicted felon who was rewarded for his or her performance at trial. How is that fair?

"Listen to this convicted felon telling us what's right and what's wrong."

I can hear them now. And you can continue to judge me based on my standings, or the choices I once made. Have that conversation. Question my motives. Judge my words. At least then, you will be able to examine your own judgement. You can see the effect of lies. And clearly, you can see the value in no longer allowing convicted felons to testify at criminal trials. Its not fair to a defendant, or the American public.

Shortly after the civil war, there was a case in California that ruled: Black Americans could not testify in court against their white counter parts. Due to it's unfair, and racial nature, the ruling was later over turned. However, there is a truly dangerous element in our justice system today that chooses to use any method available to achieve self-gratification. And our government has the power to ban this element from testifying in criminal courts, therefore, insuring fairness in all future proceedings. And unlike the days of old, this ban would not be based on the color of skin, but the content of character. These are the values our country was founded on. Fairness for all.

In closing, prisoners do not shun "snitches" because of the cooperation provided to authorities. (Not exactly) Prisoners disregard these characters, for their selfish nature and life-threatening ambitions. Its character that makes a man. *Shout out to Booker T.* And when a man has such low character that he will say or do anything to achieve his criminal goals, how can we blame others for not welcoming such a man? As a prisoner, does my life mean nothing? As a citizen, shouldn't I be protected from unfair trials and treatment? As a human being, do I not have the right to be free from threats? If so, I choose not to associate with a snitch, because a snitch is a threat to us all.

I understand that not all convicted felons are unsavory, and untrustworthy. There are wonderful people with strong morals and right-minded principles who have made mistakes, paid for those mistakes and become better people in spite of trials and tribulations. Also, there are many American citizens who were convicted unjustly, for crimes never committed. It is in light of these facts that I ask for a ban on testimony provided by convicted felons. We cannot turn back the clock. Trust me, I have tried. But we can look forward and push our nation to protect the integrity of future criminal proceedings. True fairness would not allow the possibility of a wrongful conviction. The trial standard: Beyond a reasonable doubt, will never be upheld as long as a convicted felon's word continues to be offered and accepted as evidence while his word, or the moral equalizer is denied in the jury box, voting box and grounds of government funded housing.

Our country was constructed on the foundation of ideas such as: Justice for all. In the veins of our founding fathers lived a desire to be treated fairly and equally. "When a long train of abuses and usurpations, pursuing invariably the same object evinces a design to reduce them under absolute despotism, it is their right, it is their duty to throw off such government and to provide new guards for their future security." Because, when no one else will protect you, not the building you live in, but the person, its clear that you must protect yourself. Are you still there? I hope so, because there are many "Whitey Bulgers" out there operating with immunity and catching them is not the point, because the damage is already done...

A news report pulled me from woolgathering: Inmates tried to infect themselves with the Coronavirus to get early release from prison. Los Angeles county Sheriff said the LA jail inmates had one goal in mind, get infected with the novel Coronavirus by taking turns breathing through the same mask and drinking from the same water jug.

As infections continued to spread across the country, I took another look at the screen and thought, some people will do anything to get out of jail...Facts!

CHAPTER 3

DRUG DEALERS, ADDICTS AND ABUSERS

The United States has less than five percent of the world population, and we consume two-thirds of the world's illegal drugs, and incarcerate almost a quarter of the world's prisoners. More than eight out of ten whom have some substance involvement.
-Joseph Califano Jr.
(Former US Health Secretary)

I would like to start this chapter off by stating an undisputable, unconsciously accepted, and shameful fact: America is addicted to drugs.

There are many companies, large and small, that grow, manufacture, package and ship legal and illegal drugs into the soil of American culture every single hour of every single day. Whether it's: Nicotine, Opium, Alcohol, Marijuana, Fentanyl, Poppy Seeds, Methamphetamine, Heroin, over the counter medication, under the sink concoctions, bath tub brew, artificial uppers or medically prescribed downers. Dealing in drugs is big business. Rather then face this addiction head on, or take responsibility for one's own actions, America has long chosen one enemy to constantly point the finger at. The Drug Dealer!

But not all dealers. Oh no! the legal drug dealers have permission to flood our country with intoxications of all names, for insane profit and consumer abuse. America has chosen only to blame the illegal drug dealer for her lack of discipline, and ambitions of self-destruction. Those evil peddlers who seek to escape taxation right up under Lady Liberty's powdered nose. But we all have choices to make. As a prisoner, I have been told a thousand times over, take responsibility for your own actions. So then, what of the drug user? How much longer will drug use be allowed to drive the market of supply and demand? I admit, its often easier to blame others for the issues you cause, but if we are all here taking responsibility for our own actions, let us give the drug user the floor.

I was in a United States Penitentiary located in southern Virginia, having an intellectual conversation with a notorious drug dealer from Queens, New York, who is serving a life sentence. I remember his narrative: "Fiends would be kicking my door down for the dope. I couldn't tell them no if I wanted to. They would just double their efforts, and come back more aggressive. And now I'm the villain? I never forced anyone to put that shit in they bodies."

Like it or not, he has a point. Drug users make the choice of intoxicating their own bodies to the point of dependency, then seek out the drug of choice, with no concern over the level of solicitation they are offering others to commit an actual crime. Interestingly so, the definition (according to webster) of Fiend states: Devil, Demon, an extremely wicked or cruel person, a person excessively devoted to a pursuit, Addict. And as we all know, there are millions of Americans living in poverty, punching on a glass ceiling that refuses to be compromised, while seeking better lives. There is a so-called "war on drugs" that has incarcerated millions and killed billions. But the drug dealer is not the source of the problem. I would openly argue that, the drug user is our true enemy.

But don't repeat that too loud. We must continue to whisper, because the truth hurts and the trail of mis-information leads all the way up the pyramid, to the top of our power structure. When in fact, it is the drug user that creates the illegal drug market himself. The demand for illegal drugs is driven by those that indulge in drug use. The consumer. Drug users will beg, barter, steal, fight and even murder for the type of high that will make life more bearable. Meanwhile, these "users" are often coddled by our justice system and allowed to remain in society, as drug dealers serve out numerous life sentences for yielding to their own greedy ambitions.

However, drug dealers do not create drug users. Drug users create drug dealers. Allow me to repeat that. Drug dealers do not create drug users. Drug users create drug dealers. E.g. If the sand suddenly became radio-active and humanly intoxicating, how would we know for sure? Someone would have to try it out. The user. Then once proven our sand now gives off a serious high, what do you logically see happening next? Hello!! Citizens all over the country would move faster then the 49ers to cultivate all the sand they could carry. Why? Because anything humanly intoxicating has high value (no pun intended). And that value is determined by the strength of demand. Demand: a strong request, to ask for something very strongly, to insist or require, to claim. In other words, if the people want it, it will be sold. That's the underlining truth in a capitalistic society. So why is the "Dealer" the only target?

"He is taking advantage of other people's weaknesses."

So is McDonalds, Snickers and Keefe. How can we fight a war on drugs and continue to allow the true source of the battle to remain on the field? Let's look at it from a legal stand point. Dealing in illegal drugs is a criminal offense, correct? Our justice department spends billions on drug surveillance operations in which, a "buyer" confronts a known "dealer", purchases illegal drugs then walks off as if he was never there. Why doesn't the agent move on the "buyer"? Because the target is the drug dealing scum making ill-gotten gains. But it takes at least two suspects to commit the crime of, dealing in illegal drugs. More-over, there are more than one offense being violated in a single transaction, such as, aiding and abetting, solicitation and possession. Dealing in illegal drugs is a crime, correct? Then why is the dealer the only target? Is the buyer not a willing participant in the illegal sale of drugs? Of course, he is. But law enforcement has long disregarded the user as harmless victims, craving a substance to numb reality and intensify life experiences. They don't need jail, or punishment. Thus, what they receive is our compassion. But not the dealer.

Wouldn't you consider it unfair to allow drug users to hide behind the flag, while every finger (including their own) is pointed at the dealer? The same dealer, often aggressively pursued to help fill someone's vice. Is that justice? Why does the user, who is equally responsible as the dealer, receive a slap on the wrist (bad smoker!) while the dealer is sentenced to serve serious time in prison? Haven't they committed the same crime?

Our prison system is compiled with drug dealers who were targeted by law enforcement in this so-called "war on drugs". And in four decades, the illegal sale of drugs hasn't slowed a bit. On the contrary, drug dealers have become drug users. Allow me to explain.

More than 65 percent of the 2.3 million inmates in America are substance addicts, while only 11 percent receive addiction treatment or counseling. Drug dealers of the past had strict codes against becoming users. They were motivated by being able to provide for themselves, and their loved ones. Dealers often invested their illegal funds into legitimate business. But all noble notions were pushed to the back-page or replaced with a ski-mask as the drug dealer became America's public enemy number one. By no means am I attempting to justify the drug dealer's actions or voracious thirst for cash. There have been too many lives victimized over the consensual relationship between the user and the dealer. What I attempt to illustrate is the evolution of the drug dealer from up-start to highbred.

Today's drug dealer, is also a drug user. Law enforcement have done such a wonderful job at eradicating the drug dealer of old, drug users had no choice but to pick up the laced baton. And why not? Drug users have been shielded from serving serious time, for decades.

"There are plenty of drug users, who are serving long prison terms."

A friend of mine once argued. (Hi Brook)

And she is right. But those drug users are not serving terms in prison for using drugs alone. There are other defining factors, along with drug use that equal harsh time in prison. Over all, America is soft on drug addicts.

"They need treatment, not jail."

"They have a problem."

And I agree! Their problem is our problem as a nation. Where is the sympathy for the dealer? Is his mentality such a lost cause, he deserves to spend his life in jail? What do you say about a Joe Kennedy, whose illegal actions lead to a fortune and our first Catholic President? Or, how about Shawn Carter, business man and entertainer for the ages? Are these great minds exempt from the villain tag associated with the dealer? The truth is, if you are a dealer and a user, you will most likely receive serious time.

But, if you are a drug user solely, you will most likely be home before the lights come on. (If arrested at all)

Law enforcement agents often use drug users as pellets. They send them at suspected drug dealers with no concern for their well-being. And when the suspect is arrested, the drug user is allowed to remain on the street where he will find a new supplier to serve his habit. Ultimately, there wouldn't be any new suppliers if there were no users. Sand anyone? If America decided to put down the drugs for good, the illegal market would crash. Dealer or user, we are all losing as a country by not placing responsibility evenly. Drug users are equal participants in the drug trade but not equally punished. Why? Answer anyone…because America is addicted to drugs.

The overwhelming majority of American citizen, young to old, have used some form of intoxication, at some point in life, as we frown at the baker with powder rings around our mouths and the justice system continues to target the wrong culprit. Drug addiction runs deep inside the Fabric of American society. It wreaks havoc throughout households and covers our streets abroad. Babies are having babies, parents are absent in the home, and young adults are mentally lost with no true direction. Using drugs is bad news. There are billboards, tv commercials, drug hotlines, websites, group meetings, rehab centers, motivational speakers and a long list of published books regurgitating the same message. *SAY NO TO DRUGS*.

Yet and still, drug use has reached new heights, with the legalization of weed and new spices to excite endorphins. Fentanyl is said to be Heroin on steroids. It works by flooding the brain with dopamine, creating a feeling of euphoria and relaxation. It does what Heroin does, but faster and more intensely. It can cause respiratory arrest, nausea, sedation, confusion, coma and occasionally death. The opium crisis continues to destroy lives and still we choose to get high. And why not, our role models haven't completely said no to drugs, right? Former United States Presidents, George W. Bush, Baraka Obama and Bill Clinton have all openly admitted to using cocaine or Marijuana (when it was illegal) at different points in their lives. These were the commanders of our nation. Can you feel me now? Although these men went on to lead, what most would consider decent and respectable lives, what do you suppose came of all their dealers? These are not men who can't think for themselves. These are men America elected to think for us all. And they made conscious choices to deal in illegal drugs. But only the dealer is vilified. As if the user is no real problem at all. When in fact, it is the user who creates the market for illegal drug sales, and as long as we refuse to address this truth, nothing will change.

"If we lock up all the users, there won't be anyone left."

Exactly! And that's why we have chosen to blame the drug dealer, exclusively, for our uncontrollable itch. The drug dealer is making a choice to sell to his own people. True! And the drug user is making an equal choice to purchase illegal substances. So, why are they not receiving equal time in prison? If the purpose of prison is to deter further criminal acts, where is the deterrence for the user? Surely, it can't be that stay at the "non-smoking" hotel we call treatment centers, in which guests can check themselves out. Seriously! Drug users, I'm talking strictly drug users, receive no harsh penalty for their willing part in the sale of illegal drugs. Instead, they are pampered, reasoned with, then allowed to pressure others into helping them get high. *What's the definition of Fiend again?*

But I don't expect to hear any chants of: "Lock them up!". This is simply another wake up call. Rather, I do hope that when drug users look towards the many penitentiaries in our nation, they realize that their actions help fill them up. That desire for life altering substance has created a demand for the illegal sale of drugs, which causes risk takers to reach for illegal profits and law enforcement to choose sides. Only when we finally start taking responsibility for our own actions, and stop solely blaming the candy-man for America's sweet tooth, will we truly grow as a nation. *I truly believe that.*

And I'm not over looking the fact that many Americans need powerful drugs to escape the pain of injuries. E.g. The men and women in the armed service, who I have great respect for. I understand that many drug-dependent addictions come from honest attempts to sooth the pains of our past. Realistically, drug use, both legal and illegal is here to stay, and that's why we must stop incarcerating men and women on both sides who fall short in desperate times.

The war on drugs should be fought at the heart of the problem, or not fought at all. Over 80 percent of American's 2.3 million prisoners are non-violent offenders. Prosecutors want us to believe these men and women are threats to society, and incarcerated in order to protect the public. But who will protect you from yourself? How many life terms must a drug dealer serve before we realize the true source of America's addiction? America is addicted to drugs. And as long as this fact remains, there will always be dealers. Moreover, drug users, addicts and abusers are not victims. They are willing participants in the illegal dealings of drugs. Why must we protect them and crucify the sober? I get it now, there isn't enough beds. And besides, if the users received the same punishment as the dealers, there wouldn't be any judges left to sentence them.

Drug addicts need treatment. True! But first they need to be identified. Policemen, politicians and correctional officers can not be excluded from these classifications. There are mind altering drugs that turn responsible men and women into reckless juveniles. Some are legal. Some are not. Our justice system continues to allow these offenders to escape unscathed. Consequently, many drug users do not have a criminal record. And with no method of identifying these individuals, drug users continue to get hired in law enforcing positions.

Truthfully, I do not wish incarceration on others. And we don't need to add to mass incarcerations. At times, all we need is assistance to become better people. The law should be enforced equally or not at all. Drug users should use their voice to speak out against harsh prison sentences. No one should be serving a life sentence in prison for the distribution of Marijuana. (Shout out to C.V) This is for those who insist on throwing rocks, and hiding their hands, causing pain to others while skipping out on responsibility. I hope that all drug users now understand, they are willing participants in the drug trade, and not immune to its aftermath. And with over 180,000 federal inmates, I hope we can take an honest look at the true cause of mass incarceration, once and for all. Drug dealers are not innocent. But they are not alone either. We are all in this together. So why not work together to correct it? I'll let someone else answer that…

CHAPTER 4

MENTAL ILLNESS

"620 of more than 140,000 inmates in the FBOP have tested positive, while 357 staff members have been infected."

The walls are starting to talk. Our country was dealing with a crisis like no other. I was responding to family e-mails trying to explain the last few months and understand the current situation. Inmates hustled across the "Day Room" from showers to phones. The director of FBOP had recently announced an increase of phone minutes, from 300 minutes to 500 minutes a month, to counter the shutdown of visitations for all prisoners across the system. This gesture was said to help inmates better communicate with their loved ones, throughout the troubling pandemic that was claiming American lives every day. Not long after, the Bureau decided to make all phone calls free of charge, taking the burden off all family members and prisoners alike. Firm and fair? Not quite!

My fingers were busy when I heard the guard shout: "Ellis!" I looked in his direction and noticed three more uniformed officers standing with him. As I rose to my feet, I quickly clicked off the e-mail system, not sure why I was being called.

"You Ellis?", one guard asked.

When I nodded my head in response, another guard said, "You're going to the hole".

"For what!" I disputed naturally, by then I was surrounded on all sides.

"Put your hands behind your back."

I reluctantly complied, then I felt the handcuffs clasp around my wrists. My questions received no answers as I was escorted to the special housing unit. All three officers claimed they were simply following orders, and I would have to speak with someone who received higher pay then themselves. We reached the secured door and waited for the electronic lock to give access. I noticed an empathic look on one of the guard's faces. Although he didn't say a word, it was clear to me that, whatever the cause of my sudden separation was clearly unfair, and he knew it.

The moment we entered the SHU (Special Housing Unit) area, I could smell and hear the change of environment, with indignation on my mind.

"Yeah! I got this shit for your ass." An inmate, locked in a steel holding tank shouted. "Ya'll wanna fuck with me! I'm a shit you bitches down."

After my escorts locked me in a similar cage, they removed the handcuffs and stepped away. I watched as one of them interacted with the screaming inmate.

"Hey Taylor, shut the fuck up will you."

"You shut the fuck up! I got something really good for all you crackers." The inmate continued to rant.

He was half naked and covered in human feces. He held onto the cage, and pressed his face in-between the cracks. Now, I'm no doctor but, judging the length of commitment, something seemed to be wrong with his mental state. But instead of a trained specialist, at that point, all he received was untrained antagonist. Prison guards, who are taught to meet force with force (fight fire with fire) often bring the wrong weapons. As prisoners, some find it hard to even identify clear mental decline. After all, prisons are made to punish the convicted. Right? I believe the American public deserve to know the truth. Which is, today's prison system is not a penal system at all (well, maybe by design), although the sign on the door remains the same (The Big house), the residents have long been integrated.

Starting in the 1950's, the government slowly moved thousands of mentally ill people out of asylums and hospitals. The process known as de-institutionalization has created many problems in policing throughout the system, related to health. I.E; In 1950, half million Americans lived in secured psychiatric institutions. By 2000, that number was only 50,000. And with, fifty-five percent of male inmates and seventy-three percent of female inmates suffering from mental health issues, America's prisons have become the world's largest psychiatric care provider.

There are conversations being held throughout the country over mental health. And as we all become more familiar with the often-over-looked ailments that silently effects the lives of millions, its time to take a good look at the prisoner. More than two-thirds of prisoners have mental health problems. We are learning new, and legitimate causes of mental deficiencies such as; head injuries, substance abuse and even birth defects. There are serious mental illnesses that cause behavioral problems, and break downs in brain functioning. And, as psychologists and neurologists scramble to explain what "Normal" human behavior is, more cases continue to come to light, demonstrating our over-all neglect in treating past subjects properly. But what about the inmate (Now you understand why they call us inmates)? Are inmates not confessed drug abusers? Does the convicted have a normal functioning brain? Or, do we just not care enough to find out? I mean, once you commit a crime, the result should be punishment at all cost. Right? Let's talk about it.

A lot of these so-called "inmates" are handicapped by temper tantrums, generally rude, immature, highly self-centered, arrogance and suffer from the inability to get along with others. They have a disregard for rules and regulations. Why? What if I told you that more than half of America's prisoners are currently suffering from mental illnesses? Well, I just did. And unfortunately, its true. These mental illnesses cause; black outs, irrational decisions, depression, post-traumatic stress, obscene sexual desires, paranoia, anxiety attacks, brain numbness, aggressive behavior, forgetfulness and loose associations. Do you really want to hear this? If not, here is your chance to get out, because if you could witness even half of what I have seen while living among these prisoners for over a decade, you just might begin to realize the reason behind America's recidivism rate. I'll give you a hint, the lack of mental health treatment. You see, those inmates beating on the door and covering their bodies with human waste, don't need an incident report, they need help.

E.g. Tayvon was from Virginia. I met him while serving time at USP Victorville. He was a tall, young black man serving a very long term for robbery. He was very quiet, and although he often wore a menacing look on his face, he was as soft as a teddy bear, fresh out of the dryer.

The first time I noticed he was a little "different", was during a Monday night tv session. Hundreds of prisoners gathered in the "day room" to watch their favorite program. I was seated among the crowd when Tayvon suddenly stood up, pulled his shirt from his body and started rolling his body like Magic Mike. He waved his shirt in the air like a helicopter, and never said a word. I assumed he saw something on one of the tv's that really excited him. I searched the screens with my eyes and found nothing so explosive to jump up and dance about. Then I looked back at Tayvon and saw another inmate guiding him back to his chair, with a gentle hand and an annoyed look on his face.

Other prisoners held in their laughter. Twenty minutes later, Tayvon was back on his feet with his shirt off. He funky rolled his body like he was at a disco, with no concern for all those who watched. As some pointed their fingers in his direction, the same inmate as before successfully calmed the gentle giant by guiding him back to his seat. I later found out that Tayvon suffered from a mental illness that caused him to be; easily excited, irrational thinker, flight of ideas and paranoid ideation, among other things. Even more detrimental, he often had violent seizures in the middle of the night, when he forgot to take his pills. The psychology department placed bottles in his possession to last a month to unburden themselves from calling him to medical every day. As if he seemed responsible enough to guide his own treatment.

As fate would have it, one cold night in December, I awake around 3 AM due to a cell alarm blaring throughout the unit. When I looked out my cell door window., I could see the red blinking light next to Tayvon's cell door. The duress alarm continued to sound off for another hour before the unit officer finally decided to walk from his office to the cell, which was a little over twenty feet away. When the officer turned off the alarm, and called for medical assistance, Tayvon had been dead for over an hour. He choked on his own tongue after biting down hard while suffering from a seizure. Tayvon's cellmate was subsequently thrown in the hole and placed under investigation, even though the cause of death was apparent. But its not beyond the FBOP to punish inmates for their own neglects and misconduct, now is it?

Even worse, while serving time at Victorville, Tayvon was issued numerous incident reports for actions he couldn't control, and helped maintain his presence in a system he should have never been sentenced to in the first place. Why is it that we treat our soldiers with compassion when they often return from foreign lands, then commit heinous crimes, yet prisoners like Tayvon only receive harsh punishments? An ex-soldier's mental stability is always taken into consideration (or should be), along with the crime he commits. While other offenders are most often, not treated with similar candor. In fact, prisoners who have shown themselves to be irresponsible are often asked to become their own psychiatrist while seeking rehabilitation for the commission of crimes they have yet to understand. *No wonder they self-medicate.*

Is it because we, as a people understand the psychological side affects of our war veterans, or we simply don't care about the mental health of the incarcerated? There are millions of prisoners who suffer from traumatic events while dealing with daily insults to their bodies, minds and egos. But no one seems to care about the patterns of emotional and physical abuses often caused by poverty and mental starvation. Meanwhile, prisoners are left alone to deal with illnesses and handicaps, persistent persecution and prejudice. They commit social suicide, not over indifference to their own future but out of desperation, and repeated failures as a person. Terrifying tragedies, such as traumatic deaths, rapes, mass catastrophes (Riots) and other events, often leave permanent imprints while officials dismiss them as tough prison life. Over a dozen prisoners lost lives (before Covid) while I served time at Victorville USP. How should I feel about that?

There are established laws that guard defendants from prosecution, when said defendant cannot appreciate the "right or wrong" in their own actions. That is, a mentally deficient defendant is not allowed to stand trial for crimes committed in turn, they are said to be innocent by way of insanity. This is the law. So then, how does a mentally ill person like Tayvon arrive at one of the most violent United States Penitentiaries, convicted and sentenced. You ready? The courts value punishment over treatment. We are talking "value" here. Prisons are big business and needs bodies to bank. Someone has to fill these beds.

The courts often go over and beyond to deem a defendant perfectly sane, when he or she is shown to have come from the lower heights of society. Even though, over half the prison population are illiterate, psychopathic narcissists (Note; it's an accepted fact that psychopaths cannot be cured, only managed). While our upper-class citizens are often given the full treatment: interviews, counseling and left to establish the deeper cause of their criminal behavior. Consider this:

In the early 2000's, a Massachusetts man coined "the hockey dad", beat his son's hockey coach to death with his bare fist, in front of the entire team. After conviction, the hockey dad was sentenced to six years in prison. Six years, for pounding another man's head into the cold ice. At sentencing, the court spent hours defending the man's mental state at the time of the murder.

On the contrary, a Boston man was convicted of being a felon in possession of a firearm, and given a life sentence in federal prison, in 2005. Details of the case showed that a police officer assaulted the man and pointed the gun at his head. Fearing legal assassination, the man pulled the gun from the officer and fled the scene. At trial, his mental state was never examined. A plea of self defense was not even allowed into court. Now I don't think I have to tell you who was part of upper society, and whom belongs to the lower. And I won't make this about race either. The underlining point is that our justice system is broken in ways that affect us all, directly or indirectly.

There are mentally ill prisoners serving long prison terms with no true understanding of their own actions. That alone gives weight to the fact that they are prone to committing the same acts in the future. Inside the prison system, similar to the courts, these clear signs of mental illness and self-destruction are ignored. Why? Because if we acknowledge any of these symptoms, over half the prison population would be placed in treatment centers, where they belong. And we can't do that. Oh no, the big business of costly prisons would drop, not to mention the employment rate. Many would rather forget that most of these convicted men and women do not have a high school diploma, G.E.D. or social skills. They lack emotional intelligence and control of their own impulses. Often depressed, unable to function, insecure and nonconforming. Some are individuals who accept little responsibility for their actions or behaviors, defend themselves by being hostile or withdrawn, immature and antisocial. But who cares about that stuff, they committed crimes, right?

"If so many prisoners are mentally incompetent, how are they able to defend their actions?"

Good questions! Everyone has a natural instinct to protect the psychological self, in much the same way we protect our physical self. The same as we will go to great lengths to protect our bodies from harm, we also seek to protect our self-image. When the physical self is threatened, we engage in what is called the "fight or flight" response. Similarly so, when the psychological self is threatened the mind engages in what is called the "accept or deflect" response.

There are many different levels of mental illness. Repression of depression causes the denial of the inability to cope with depression and mental health issues. Shaming and blaming individuals that try to get help undiagnosed exacerbates problems and often lead to incarceration itself. Pride alone can stop many of men from accepting the fact their own brain isn't functioning correctly. Whether we admit it or not, the defunction becomes evident when we continue to harm ourselves, and others with no conscious of correcting our wrongs.

Now whose job is it to screen these prisoners for potential mental illnesses while incarcerated? That would be The Mental Health services. How is it possible, to even entertain the thought of so many mentally ill prisoners walking around untagged without the Administration's knowledge? Oh, they know! They just don't care. I direct your attention to the Federal Bureau of Prisons: Purpose and scope

This program statement provides policy, procedures, standards, and guidelines for the delivery of mental health services to inmates with mental illness in Federal Bureau of Prison Correction Facilities. For the purpose of the Program statement, mental illness is defined as in the most current Diagnosis and Statistical Manual of Mental Disorders: "A mental disorder is a syndrome characterized by clinically significant disturbance in an individual's cognition, emotion regulation, or behavior that reflects a dysfunction in the psychological, biological, or developmental processes underlying mental functioning. Mental disorders are usually associated with significant distress or disability in social, occupational, or other important activities."

Classification of an inmate as seriously mentally ill requires consideration of his/her diagnosis, the severity and duration of his/her treatment history and current treatment needs. Mental illness not listed below may be classified as seriously mentally ill on a case-by-case basis if they result in significant functional impairment.

The following diagnoses are generally classified as serious illnesses:

Schizophrenia spectrum and other Psychotic disorders

Bipolar and related disorders

Major depression disorders

In addition, the following diagnoses are often classified as serious mental illnesses, especially if the condition is sufficiently severe, persistent, and disabling:

Anxiety disorders

Obsessive-compulsive and related disorders

Trauma and stressor related disorders

Intellectual disabilities and autism spectrum disorders

Major neuro-cognitive disorders

Personality disorders

TEAM APPROACH TO CARE

Due to their potential vulnerability in a correctional setting, inmates with mental illness may require special accommodation in areas such as housing, discipline, work, education, designations, transfers, and re-entry to unsure their optimal functioning. The Bureau uses a team approach to unsure the needs of inmates with mental illness are identified and addressed.

The institution Care Coordinator (CCare) and Re-entry Team is a multidisciplinary team that uses a holistic approach to ensure critical aspects of care for inmates with mental illness are considered and integrated. It is a required component at all Care2-MH, Care3-MH, and Care4-MH institutions. It is not required at pretrial facilities or Federal Transfer Centers.

The CCare Team identifies potential concerns affecting inmates with mental illness in a correctional environment, such as:

Mental health symptoms that are unreported or unidentified by the inmate.

Housing problems or cellmate conflicts.

Work and/or leisure time deficits.

Criminal thinking and behavior.

Bullying or abuse by other inmates.

Escalating patterns of destructive or dangerous behavior.

The CCare Team also identifies strategies and supports to mitigate potently negative interactions between inmates with mental illness and the correctional environment, such as:

Positive reinforcement (Cell-mates, positive staff relationships, spiritual community, mental health companion program)

Housing accommodations.

Meaningful ways to spend time (Work, supported employment, recreation, drop-in groups).

The CCare Team considers how these strategies and supports might be applied to improve funding and enhance opportunities for recovery. Meetings are ordinarily held no less than once a month and may be held in conjunction with the SHU meeting.

Every Care4-MH inmate is reviewed by the team at least quarterly. Every Care3-MH inmate is reviewed by the team as needed at least semi-annually. Care2-MH inmates are reviewed by the team as needed and at least annually. If an inmate participates in a residential PTP, his/her case may be staffed in that setting at the discretion of the Mental Health Treatment Coordinator.

Sounds really professional, doesn't it? That's about all it does. In truth, inmates with documented mental illness, who ask for a cellmate change in order to avoid conflict are sent away and told to work it out. Prisoners are forced into "mental health companion programs" without pay (or knowledge of the program itself). And those "escalating patterns of destruction or dangerous behavior", staff members create them by verbally provoking the mentally unstable and violently subduing them afterwards. The Mental Health Services' purpose and scope (there is a lot more information to this section provided by Prisoner's Rights and Lexis Nexis Group) fails to mention one known fact. All staff members must act as correctional officers first and foremost. That means psychology department heads also, which equals: Punishment before treatment, force before help and security over the needs of all inmates. Its prison, what do you expect? But this order causes a conflict between a psychologist's job and their assigned duty. Therefore, psychologists have become accommodationists. I.E, they identify the issue but never promote a solution. They maintain a stern approach when dealing with an inmate and only offer methods of coping with misfortune. "I'm on fire!" Tell me how that feels.

But this approach causes tension between the patient and the nurse. More-over, members of the psychology department are taught to see prisoners as less than human. We are cases, numbers ready to be filed away, or completely disregarded. Psychologists are trained to ignore a prisoner's complaints unless there is visible evidence such as, blood on the floor or cuts around the skin.

"Prisoners will say anything to get one over on staff."

What about the ones that are truly suffering? The FBOP answers with drugs and work packets that continue to encourage prisoners to accept the mistreatment and injustice as a way of life. Prison is not a nice place to live. This solution, although not a solution, is convenient for staff members, but disastrous for the prisoner.

Let me explain:

I once sat down with the head of the mental health services department at Hazelton USP, to be interviewed, after being placed in the Special Housing Unit. I explained the stress and depression I felt from spending so much time in solitary confinement. I also complained about the staff, and what I saw as unfair treatment. The head of the department looked me straight in the eyes and said, "Don't come to jail".

But this is only a small example of the on-going indifference instilled into prison workers throughout the system. Their training, or lack thereof, comes from the top, and the message to prisoners is clear; we don't give a damn about your gripes. Instead of addressing issues head-on, pulling up co-workers and correcting unfair and often cruel actions, psychology staff members are taught to act as correctional officers first: protect staff, and the building. Ignore frivolous inmate concerns. Therefore, prisoners receive mental health care that is inconsistent with FBOP policy concerning "serious mental ill" inmates. And who classifies these inmates? Well, they do of course. *No blood no foul.*

In addition, no psychology staff member or correctional officer (same thing in today's system) wants to be labeled a "Hug-a-thug", or soft on inmates. This could potentially result in back-lashes from fellow workers (social acceptance). And possibly, the loos of a job (job security). These phobias are part of the reason why a prisoner's needs will always come second to staff members, in this system that views human beings as numbers or cases, to be controlled and pushed to the side. Consequently, mental illness is dismissed as bad behavior while the prison population continues to suffer from over sights and slights.

I grew up battling dyslexia. My educational years were spent in special education classes. I never read a book in its entirety until I was twenty-three years old. Were these facts considered at my sentencing? Not at all! I was handed a 27-year term for a victimless crime, without even a single nod to the 20 years of law-abiding citizenship. Dyslexia encompasses a far wider range of language disorders. Some dyslexics have difficulty processing sound, others have trouble processing the visual word, while others find it difficult to extract meaning from pointed words. But the courts don't want to hear about learning disabilities. Why not? Because, if we are considered to learn slower than others, and often mis-comprehend what is read, then the level of "full responsibility" is lowered, and might even require some compassion. And for a country, committed to a tough on crime approach, we just can't have that. Now can we?

The FBOP trains its workers to look away from mental health issues, so that, the only response to mis-conduct will be punishment. E.g. little Ray was a former cellmate of mine. He was sentenced to ten years for possession of a firearm. At sentencing, the judge asked him why he felt the need to carry a gun, and Little Ray responded, he carried a gun because he was shot nine times in his neighborhood and wanted to protect himself from being shot again. Did I mention Little Ray was only 19 and about 5,2 and 119 lbs? Despite the honesty in his explanation, Little Ray was given ten years for "attempting" to protect his own life. And there are thousands of prisoners who share similar stories. They start off with a victim of violent acts. The survivors decide to protect themselves from future harm. Their brains are re-wired to risk going to jail (where it's often safer for them). multiple times, rather then lose their lives obeying the laws of the land. There is only one mission: stay alive.

If this was one of our soldiers returning from war, it would easily be classified as Post Traumatic Stress Disorder. But for a young man living in a dangerous city block, it's easier to label him a criminal without any real consideration for the mental illnesses that continue to cause his illegal actions. I said "continues to cause". The fear of being severely injured doesn't just disappear once he arrives in prison. Oh no! the trauma continues while psychologist focus on punishment over help or treatment. And although there are thousands of inmates suffering from similar plights, the truth is they should not even be here.

Prisons were not constructed to serve as mental institutions. Thanks to de-institutionalization, there are very few mental help providers and a shit load of prisons. Inmates with mental health issues are labeled "sane" and placed in general population where they are punished repeatedly for unchecked mental disfunctions. Case and point.

I received another cellmate in the fall of 2016. After reading his "paperwork" I realized he had a long history of being victimized in violent acts. He was sentenced to fifteen years, for possession of a firearm while in commission of a robbery. After four months in prison, he received five incident reports, all for weapon possession. One day, he was return-ing to our cell after another short stay in solitary confinement, and I decided to sit him down for a talk.

"Why you always got a joint on you?" I asked

"I don't feel right without it." He answered.

"Have you ever stabbed anyone?"

"Never!"

"Do you want to stab someone?"

"Not at all."

"Then why continue to carry a weapon, and chance receiving write up after write up?" I asked.

He looked me straight in the eyes, "I rather be caught with it than without it."

He was a non-violent offender. A man who was victimized by vio-lence, but never committed any himself. And regardless of the amount of solitary confinement, loss of privileges and "good time" credit taken away, he would continue to carry at all cost. *PTSD anyone.* I was told that the number one law of human nature is self-preservation. If this is true, why must a men spend decades behind bars for carrying (not using) a weapon he believes might one day save his own life?

There are no scare tactics that will change his mind state. He is al-ready scared. There is no jail sentence that will deter him from being concerned about his own safety. He needs treatment, not punishment. I have read hundreds of prisoner's background history and over 90% of them started using drugs at an early age, almost admittedly after being victimized by a violent assault. Where's the help? The administration is too concerned with being fair and firm, but is it fair to ignore the clear brain malfunctions causing prisoners to scream out for long periods of time throughout a day, pull out their private parts at the sight of a wom-an, injure themselves often for attention, shower ten times a day, place other people's spit in their mouths, cover their body with feces or act out until their bodies shut down? Or is the mission to break down our self-esteem?

"By definition, low self-esteem means a person does not feel in con-trol. Self-respect comes from self-control. By circumstance robbing a person of his freedom takes away his vestige of control. In effect, it harms his sole source of self-esteem and causes him to lash out. He is at the mercy of the world to make him feel good, so he fights, defending his ego and justifying his beliefs, values and actions, as well as his right to be heard. He already feels out of control, so he will defend every last drop of true freedom he can maintain."

-David J. Lieberman PHD

Award winning author, internationally recognized

leader in the field of human behavior

I have witnessed prisoners with symptoms of ADHD, PTSD, OCD, learning disabilities and legitimate psychological illnesses congregate among other violent prisoners as if there is no difference in brain functioning or concern for safety, all in the name of mass incarceration, in a system that values punishment over treatment.

"I don't know how you remain sane after all these years." A friend of mine once asked?

In truth, the answer is, you don't! there have been many nights that my mental stability was pushed to the limit. My vision was clouded by anger and frustration for being dismissed or disrespected. But when the smoke clears, the truth remains: when no one will protect you from harm, it's best to start helping yourself.

Unfortunately, there are thousands of prisoners suffering from mental illnesses that continue to go untreated, or simply ignored, who are less able to focus on the reality of their own situations and properly adapt in order to find solutions. Some prisoners only seek methods to escape reality, and the psychology department is pretty good at supplying medication. Numb the brain, keep the prisoners breathing, but don't teach him too much. For those seeking help or a better life, that's simply not the agenda at this time. A correctional officer's manifesto is: Every day is a good day with pay, and no inmate getting in the way. Or so I have heard.

But if we are talking about criminal justice reform, with "reform" being the key word, we have to start looking at the real problems, instead of turning a blind eye while others fatten their own pockets. I truly hope that these psychology staff members find the courage to speak out against cruel practices, they know are morally and ethically wrong. Having a job and paying your bills is responsible, but if your job is to deny treatment (not just stabilize minds) to the mentally ill, the question becomes, what are you truly being paid to do? And what about the smaller percentage of prisoners who do not suffer from mental health issues? Where is the protection for them? Is there any concern for their well-being while in-carcerated with a psychotic cell-mate, or suicidal bunkie?

The FBOP forces inmates to "cell-up" with other prisoners, regard-less of the well documented mental illnesses one or the other might have. In fact, when an inmate has shown himself to be suicidal, self-mutilating, sociopathic, uneasy and full of anxiety, the administration recommends a cell-mate. Not a mental health companion (inmates paid to pair with the mentally ill). But, another prisoner to place in harm's way. These actions not only ignore an inmate's cry for help, they also place other inmate (of-ten unknowingly) in danger. If a prisoner is suicidal, what will stop him from taking his cell-mate's life along with his own?

Prison officials have long turned over the keys to prisoner mental health, by neglecting their own jobs and leaving the incarcerated to figure it out. Inmates are forced to become cell-mates in order to watch each other and perform duties that officers are paid to provide. I'm no doctor. It's not my business to talk another inmate off the ledge. Or is it? In do-ing so, my life is constantly placed in jeopardy every single day. Prisoners are not allowed to view other prisoner's mental records, but the psychol-ogy department know very well who they are placing together, and what might come of it. These experiments often end in blood shed, incident reports and loss of privileges. But that's how the game is played.

As a country, we have a lot to do, rather fix. But a true conversation is a bridge way to a real understanding. Moreover, if our justice system continues to overlook the mentally ill by piling them into prisons instead of treatment center, a cycle of victimization will continue to hurt us all. Punishment has replaced professional assistance, as sanity continues to drown in a pool of prescription drugs where everyone looks alike. But we are not. We are different, and it's time to take action differently. *You think?*

CHAPTER 5

THE SHU

—◦⟨⟨⟩⟩◦—

After two months in the Special Housing Unit (SHU), news spread fast about the number of infected prisoners within the FBOP. I learned that several inmates had died in our facilities across the country. More alarming to me was the fact that my home town of Boston Mass. Was especially struck hard by the pandemic. Worried about my family's safety, I argued with staff members to allow me the proper means of communication. While in the SHU, inmates are not allowed to use the email system or make frequent phone calls. We are locked inside our cells twenty-four hours a day, with the exception of one hour recreation in a steel cage located in the facility. Recreation was canceled until further notice, and commissary items were limited to hygiene products only. No pen nor paper was issued to the prison population for months. And to that point, I was still denied a reason for being placed in the hole.

I pondered on why I was being treated so unfairly, and punished without a cause. Due process was thrown out the window. As a prisoner, I wouldn't be rewarded an explanation for being further separated from my loved ones at a time of a national crisis. Every day I tried to maintain a certain level of calm as the worst thoughts entered my mind: Has something happened to my family? Are they holding me in solitary confinement to control my response? After all that I suffered at Lompoc, I did not understand why the administration at Victorville would suddenly place me back in the SHU. It didn't make sense. Officers often joked that the FBOP stands for Fucking Backwards on Purpose. As I searched my mind for rational reason, at that time, I had to agree.

Similar to the compound, special housing unit holds many unsavory prisoners. "Checkins" are inmates who refuse to be on the yard, due to the risk of injury or fear of other prisoners. They are often smug individuals; due to the protection the administration provides them. Interestingly enough, they are often disliked by staff and other inmates. "Gunners" are super-sexed inmates, who cannot control their sexual urges. Their obscene actions tend to run a foul by staff and convicts alike. "Gang bangers" seek to claim territory, and increase their numbers. "Drug Addicts" sleep all day and irritate others all night. But it's the "mentally ill" that crowd the hole, and command the most attention, with arguments, fights and disruptions. When I arrived, I requested a single cell. I pointed out the current crisis and the need for social distancing. One infected prisoner could quickly become two if forced to "cell-up" with others. Needless to say, my concerns were denied. The FBOP forces prisoners to cell with other prisoners, Coronavirus or not.

I was threatened with disciplinary action if I refused, and considering the circumstances, I didn't want to legitimize the administration's illegal actions by giving them reason to hold me in the SHU. So, I allowed them to place me in a cell with another prisoner, and tried to maintain my resolve over the shouts and banging coming from all sides. The special housing unit consists of multiple ranges, with cells lined up on both sides, down a narrow hallway. The officers in special housing unit are more aggressive, more abusive and completely numb to legitimate complaints coming from the prisoners. They go jab for jab and penalize everyone for one inmate's actions.

I was placed in a cell with a man from Texas. After we were introduced, I noticed a blank stare in his eyes. It was like, he was physically standing in front of me, but mentally traveling the universe. *Drug Addict.* I was given the run down on clothing, toilet paper, toothbrushes and blankets. Inmates become more comfortable with familiarity. In the hole, the administration visits once a week during what they call "SHU Rounds", I had spoken with the assistant warden about my situation, and he promised me answers on his next round. So, when I heard prisoners shouting from their cells, calling out department figure's names, I hoped to receive what I had coming.

"A.W!", I called out behind the glass window.

When he stopped to speak with me, the first thing I noticed was the mask covering his mouth. A quick look over his shoulder, and I took note of other staff members wearing similar face covers. It was the middle of May, and inmates in the special housing unit at Victorville were yet to receive face covering. I abandoned my thoughts and spoke directly: "So why am I in the SHU?"

"It was the new warden's call." Said the A.W

"But I'm on hold over status, what does the Warden have to do with it?"

"He just told us to place you in SHU."

"Where did this new Worden come from?" I asked.

The A.W lifted his eyes and said," I believe he just left USP Lompoc."

Mystery solved. The new Warden at Victorville was the same Warden who over saw the mistreatment at Lompoc. My sudden "SHU" placement was further retribution for exercising my administrative remedy rights, over staff misconduct at Lompoc. The "Beef" had followed me; and now the Warden was exercising his power in retaliation. I shook my head, but before I could ready a response the A.W spun his head around in the opposite direction. A uniformed officer was arguing with another inmate after opening his tray slot to hand him an envelope full of legal papers.

"I need to call my family." The inmate shouted, while holding the slot open with his forearm.

"I'm giving you a direct order." The guard responded.

"I just need to speak to my family. We haven't had the phone in weeks."

"The officer told you to release tray slot." The A.W got involved.

Soon there were officers and administration staff members surrounding the cell. The inmate tried to explain his situation. He was losing custody of his only child and begged for a phone call to stop the courts from ruling out his testimony. But the firm never fair rule was kicking into over drive.

"This is your last chance.", one officer threatened.

When the inmate asked to speak to the psychologist, the staff members had heard enough. They left the range one at a time, visibly angry. I could see the inmate mumbling to himself. His frustration exploded into words as the teer flooded with profane verbal support.

"I got mental issues for real!", he shouted. "My shit documented! I don't give a fuck! You ain't goin' to fuck with my family!"

There was silence on the teer long enough for another prisoner to offer his words.

"Yo, they suiting up out there bro."

Remember the hammer and nail analogy? Prison officials seem to value violence as their ultimate weapon. Not to rehabilitate. What's that? Violence is used to subpress, subdue, and control. Forty minutes passed, then eight heavily armed

"officers" marched down the range, all in riot gear and ready to work. The lead guard held a shield bigger than his body. He was flanked by two guards holding paintball guns. The SHU Lieutenant had a M.90 aimed at the open slot. The inmate saw the high-powered weapons pointed in his direction and retreated to the back of his cell.

"Cuff up!", the Lieutenant ordered.

"Fuck you!", A voice shouted from the back of the teer.

Now honestly, if regaining control of the tray slot was the mission, the inmate was clearly nowhere near the damn thing. The lieutenant could have shut it, and secured a victory without the use of force. But that would have been too simple, and they didn't get all dressed up for nothing. I heard the Lieutenant say, "The inmate is refusing to cuff up." Then "Pop! Pop! Pop!". The shots were followed by designed chaos. Inmates kicked their doors and banged food trays against the glass. "Pop! Pop! Pop!". "Cuff up!"

Sponge rounds, tipped with stiff foam, flew into the room. Pepper spray spread to every cell. I pressed a wet towel against my nose as my cellmate coughed uncontrollably. "Cuff up!"

I could see over top of the goon squad. The inmate was not in view. From the angles of the shots fired, I guesstimated he was most likely under the bed bunk. *That's where I would have been.* Although defenseless and completely outnumbered, the administration expected a job to be carried out, and that was an order soldier. So, the Lieutenant threw a stun grenade inside a sealed 8x10 cell to flush out a defenseless (most likely scared) inmate. "Boom!"

The walls rattled. Correctional officers took turns trying their weapons. After ten minutes of battle, I questioned whether the prisoner was still alive. Then I saw a shivering wrist extending outside of the open slot. The inmate was handcuffed and drug off the range coughing and spitting on the floor. He wasn't the only one. The gas unleashed entered the ventilation system and caused similar reactions to every prisoner in the special housing unit. *Over a phone call.*

It has been reported that tear gas and pepper spray can wreak havoc on the body. If exposed to tear gas or pepper spray, it's effects can typically begin within seconds, and last up to an hour. Those with health issues such as, asthma or a weak heart can have possible long-lasting health effects. Eye pain and temporary blindness, disoriented thoughts, panic attacks. If inhaled, pepper spray may also cause sudden elevation of blood pressure, which can precipitate a stroke or heart attack, burning nasal cavity, runny nose, dry cough, gagging and difficulty speaking. Your skin can feel like it is on fire and blisters may form. I have watched inmates vomiting after being "teamed" by over anxious officers ready to try their new weapons. And for what? *Over a phone call.* Wouldn't it have been easier to allow the inmate a ten-minute call? "Oh no, then we would have to do it for everyone" so then, you rather give everyone the gas instead? Re-training is a must. Correctional officers have to learn "conflict resolution" skills.

The next morning, I heard a commotion in front of my cell door. Another inmate claimed his mother had just fallen victim of the deadly virus. He was screaming at the duty officer to let him out of the cell. When the officer refused, the inmate covered his window with tissue.

"Uncover your window!", the officer ordered.

After repeating himself numerous times, the officer then said, "You ain't getting shit talking to me like that. Now if you do things the right way, I will help you".

"Fuck that! My mother just died and I don't give a shit about nothing. Fuck You!"

"You're the one that's going to lose. We will just team your ass." The officer walked off the range as the banging started up, in support of the grieving prisoner.

The noise echoed throughout the special housing unit, and other ranges full of prisoners joined in. "Board up! Board up!" Inmates shouted. A lieutenant showed up (not a psychologist) for a last attempt at negotiation. When the inmate explained that he was ready to hurt himself. The Lieutenant responded, "Aw man, you need a cellmate." *Really?* Once the Lieutenant left the range there would be no more negotiating. Another "team" moved on the cell in similar fashion to those before it. The inmate never received the help he was clearly acting out for. Instead, he got a face full of gas. I have had a front row seat while inmates demanded medication or refused to take a cellmate, only to receive the gas. The administration claims their actions are justified by "taking back the cell". And some would like to believe that this is the exception. But unfortunately, it's not. Within thirty days of being placed in the special housing unit at Victorville USP, during the Coronavirus crisis that claimed more than 400,000 American lives, I witnessed over 50 of these "cell extractions".

That's close to two a day. O.C filled the air, causing watery eyes and loud coughing throughout the night. I said "continued coughs". Yes! Which is one of the major ways to contract and spread the virus that was sweeping the nation at the time. These "correctional officers" brought force to every minor dispute. They unloaded cans of spray and fired rubber bullets into a small cell to force the desired action out of prisoners. You would think such actions would be re-evaluated in a time where excessive coughing put others at serious risk. But even when a prisoner's life is in danger, the facility comes first.

Let's not forget that a lot of these prisoners have serious mental issues, that often go unchecked or untreated. The SHU only helps to make these issues worse. Our brains do not register much difference between physical pain and psychological pain. The administration took all normal privileges from every inmate placed in the special housing unit. We were only allowed one phone call a month, which added to stress and depression. Without any true outlets, the inmate population becomes restless and confused. Punishment, no rewards. Control, no treatment. With all the money poured into the prison system, the question has to be, where is the help for the incarcerated? To once again quote behavior specialist David J. Lieberman:

In the person who feels disrespected or out of control, a lack of self-respect causes an out-of-proportion response to any situation. The world, funneled through his ego is his only source of psychological nourishments. When he feels he is not getting the respect he craves, anger-the ego's ultimate weapon- engages as a defense mechanism against feelings of vulnerability, spiraling further and further from emotional health. He does not understand that the angrier he is, the less in control he becomes.

America's prisons are desperate for justice. Men and women, suffering from depression, panic attacks, hypertension, post-traumatic stress, mental anguish, and suicidal thoughts are not allowed to be human. Correctional officers cause conflict, then used said conflict to neglect the prison population from their rights promised by the constitution. Inmates are resulting to outlandish cries for help, only to receive bully tactics, abuse, aggression and punishment. We are told to file grievances that have slim chance of making it out of the building, while being ignored by the outside world, due to our inmate's name tags. The use of involuntary confinement has to be re-examined, re-evaluated and re-imagined.

Social isolation, grief, fear and uncertainty are pervasive, and have long-term mental health consequences, including leading to diagnosable conditions.

-(APA) American Psychological Association

Senior health director of health care innovation, Vaile Wright

I ask again, where is the help for the incarcerated? Psychology staff members are often a part of the goon squad that issues cans of gas to inmate's faces while being extracted from a cell he was forced into. We don't need puzzles, we need treatment. Meanwhile, a lot of prisoners are returning to society straight from the special housing units, where they have suffered months of psychological torture. Restraints do not change behavior, and abuse does not reform. Prisoners often return home worse than they left and with no restraints to hold back their mental issues. The FBOP creates resentment, not rehabilitation. Prisoners (like myself) are placed in the SHU for no clear reason, stripped of family communication and support, then forced to babysit suicidal cellmates, with no regard for safety or justice. A plea for help is answered with violence. Refuse to take a celly, Gas! Acting out over no recreation, Gas! You "boarding up" because you want toilet paper, Gas!

Extraction teams are ordered to take action over petty issues, and when they arrive, the only goal is to apply force. Which means, another O.C (oleoresin capsicum) bath for the inmate whether right or wrong. It is well known that solitary confinement causes long term psychological disorders because of serious psychological distress and high risk of going on to develop clinical diagnosis. Yet and still, it is the norm even today throughout the FBOP.

The center for Disease Control and Prevention set out ways to protect against gas when over exposed. They recommend immediately leaving the area and getting to fresh air quickly. But for the prisoners confined to a cell, in the special housing unit (SHU), this is impossible. I have had pepper spray for breakfast, lunch and dinner, while trapped in a cell with no air circulation. These chemicals were designed to control wild bears, not distraught human beings. Where is the concern for the prisoner when we are left coughing, sneezing and wiping our eyes while officers escape to fresh air, after unleashing dangerous gases?

Constitutional Rights of Prisoners

6.1: Introduction

Prison administrators have always faced the task of maintaining order and discipline in a prison. Some means of dealing with prisoners who violate instructional rules and regulations are required. One such means is the use of punitive isolation, which is isolation from the general population imposed or a penalty for violating institutional rules. Almost every correctional institution included a special confinement unit for those who misbehave seriously after they are incarcerated. This prison within a prison usually is a place of solitary confinement.

Conditions of Confinement in the SHU

541.31 Conditions of Confinement in the SHU

Your living conditions in the SHU will meet or exceed standards for heathy and humane treatment, including, but not limited to, the following special conditions:

Environment. Your living quarters will be well-ventilated, adequately lighted, appropriately heated, and maintained in a sanitary condition.

Cell occupancy. You living quarters will ordinarily house only the number of occupants for which it is designed. The Warden, however, may authorize more occupants so long as adequate standards can be maintained.

Clothing. You will receive adequate institution clothing, including footwear, while housed in the SHU. You will be provided necessary opportunities to exchange clothing and or have it washed.

6.3.3 Purpose of Isolation Confinement

In addition to granting relief on the basis of the conditions of isolated confinement, federal courts have also found a violation of the Eighth Amendment when the punishment is imposed for an improper purpose. The courts view the proper purpose of isolated confinement to be the maintenance of order within the constitution. Therefore, any punishment that is not necessary to maintain order is cruel and unusual and prohibited by the Eighth Amendment.

Why was I placed in the SHU again? The Bureau recognizes that an inmate's health may deteriorate during a restrictive housing placement. Yet they still do it. More than two-thirds of American prisoners have mental health problems. Yet, these problems are never met with true psychological help (Not puzzles either), only forced control. While in the SHU, officers control the lights, hygiene products, clothes, writing materials and meals. The administration only allowed five letters a week, which is 20 a month during a global crisis. The meals were less from what compound inmates received, making isolation even harder to deal with. This type of abuse hurts family ties and punishes without any thought of due process. Inmates can be placed in SHU for "Investigation" whenever the administration feels it necessary (or not). These so-called "investigations" can last years without ever producing a write up for rule violations. These actions are what lead to inmate hunger strikes, slot jacking, window blocking, teer flooding and shit throwing. Yeah, shit throwing. Desperation breeds mistakes.

The administration creates problems, then uses said problem as an excuse to deny the prisoners.

"Where is the mail?"

"We got busy. Go to sleep!"

None of these actions make prisons or prisoners safer. But prisoner's safety is not the goal. E.g. Inmates "check-in" for fear of their own lives and are forced to receive three incident reports before they can be officially transferred. That is, before the administration will send them to another facility, where they can be safe, they are given three chances to return to the feared compound situation. Every denial is an incident report for refusing to program. Where's the love?

I have been forced to share a cell in "solitary confinement" along inmates with antisocial personality disorders, paranoid schizophrenic disease, psychopaths and sociopaths, with no concern for my safety or theirs. Prisoners with mental health issues are constantly placed in the SHU, provoked to act out, then punished. Even though the dangers of solitary confinement are well known. Former presidents have stated that more than 30 days in solitary confinement is unjust. But the FBOP has clearly ignored them. I have spent over nine months in the special housing unit. That's over 270 days without cause or reason. These tactics are used to provoke, and once I receive an incident report, they will use it to justify my long stay. (For the record, I haven't had an incident report in over two years. And still, I suffer) Prisoners don't matter. They are made to suffer, then we release them to the public (most of them).

Operations were shut down during the last week of May. No phone calls were allowed and the mail was delayed. In an attempt to make sense of the silent drama, officers finally handed out face masks for the inmate population. However, staff members were a no-show. Each day passed with speculation in the air. We later learned about a police shooting. FBOP officers were called to help subdue the protestors. And as the Coronavirus continue to gain speed, the FBOP posted updates of their commitment in protecting the staff and the inmate population. But their assistance in the streets, all over the country had brought the virus right to us all. *Imagine that.*

CHAPTER 6

FAMILY TIES

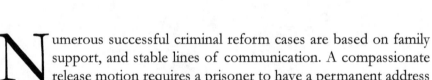

Numerous successful criminal reform cases are based on family support, and stable lines of communication. A compassionate release motion requires a prisoner to have a permanent address upon release, along with care takers, to look after the ex-offender. Prison programming includes points for maintaining family connections, ranging from poor-great. The inmate hand book states that: The Federal Bureau of Prisons encourages strong family ties, and community connections. Unfortunately, I must report that this is yet another Hallmark card created to help institutions appear more civil. The truth is, the Federal Bureau of Prisons go over and beyond to break family ties and disconnect prisoners from community connections. There are thousands of ex-offenders sent to halfway houses, with no stable residence of caring family members to return home to. A long prison term is not only hard on a prisoner, but also his loved ones, who attempt to support him as each day of his life passes by. And although the FBOP offer warm sentiments, their actions tell a different story.

Inmate family ties, along with community connections are sabotaged by FBOP administration and staff members. A prisoner's love for his family is ruthlessly used against him, to punish and cause further heartache. Prisoners are restricted from using: telephones, e-mail and visitation privileges after being found guilty of often frivolous incident reports, and sometimes before any guilt is established. But these "sanctions" are not executed solely to hurt the prisoner, they are designed to destroy family support.

Prisoners can be sanctioned for trivial actions such as, littering, or serious infractions like: fighting. Disciplinary officers have the authority to cut off communication avenues between a prisoner and his outside support system, with a stroke of his pen. But their "punishments" do not motivate a post traumatic knife carrying inmate to no longer fear for his own safety. However, it will encourage loved ones to move on with their own lives, due to lack of communication and reasonable connection through separation. Firm and fair? Allow me to offer one of my own personal experiences, as evidence to a cruel system of tactical division.

I arrived at Berlin Federal Correctional Institute in the summer of 2013. After a competitive basketball game, an inmate approached me with a verbal assault that ended with his mouth closed, and his back flat on the gym floor. The inmate was known to be a golden gloves boxing champion, and I quickly interpreted his signs of aggression to be a threat on my life. The following day, I was placed in the special housing unit for "fighting". After pleading my case to the DHO, I was found guilty, and sentenced to six months in solitary confinement, fifty-four days loss of good time, four months loss of phone use, store privileges, visits and e-mail use. These punishments felt excessive for going one round with the champ, but punishment is often over served by the FBOP with vicious intent. And they weren't finished.

In addition to my sanctions, the administration decided to transfer me over 3,000 miles away from my family. I struggled with explaining to my ten-year-old daughter (still do) why she could no longer see me, due to my new location and the lack of financial funds to travel such a long distance. Why did she have to suffer because of my actions? Wasn't an incarcerated father enough to deal with emotionally? What message is being delivered to prisoners by inflicting such damaging blows to the fabric of family support, and positive communication? "Do as we say or lose your family." That's cold. I spent over seven years in California, struggling to maintain a healthy bond with my child while navigating a foreign environment. Birthdays, holidays and special events were not spent in the visiting hall enjoying the warmth of a family that loves me, but in my cold cell, wondering how to hold onto my own sanity.

By stripping a prisoner of his communication outlets, we are not just punishing them. There are many family members who suffer from the sanctions of separation without ever even being accused of a rule violation. The first step act ruled that FBOP prisoners will be placed within 500 miles of their release address. Yet, prisoners continue to be shipped further and further away from their support systems. "It's a disciplinary transfer." Staff members attempt to justify. But who is being disciplined? Who are the real targets of these "out-of-reach" transfers? The answer is silently clear.

Families drive hours to arrive on visitation days with numerous sets of clothes in their trunk, in order to satisfy the constantly changing rules of each institution. The FBOP website gives instructions, and provides examples to show visitors what they cannot wear, but these websites are often not in agreement with the officers working behind the front desk to visitation: for example:

Mrs. Taylor attempted to visit her grandson at Lompoc USP. She arrived in a rental car, paid for at the airport near Los Angeles. She had been up for hours, and after flying in from Florida, all she wanted was to spend some time with her loved one. She went over all the proper procedures in her head as she stepped into the lobby wearing blue jeans and white shirt, with a colorful garment covering her attire. When she approached the desk, the "officer" informed her that she could not enter the visiting hall. After taking note of the shocked look on Mrs. Taylor's face, the officer informed her she couldn't wear open toed sandals. Frustrated and reasonably upset, Mrs. Taylor traveled to a local store and returned for the second time wearing black boots. Then the officer told her that she couldn't enter due to the colors in her garment. Mrs. Taylor tried an additional two times to enter the visiting hall with no avail. When her outfit was finally approved from head to toe, Mrs. Taylor was told that visitation hours were coming to a close. She did not get to see her grandson on that day, despite her every effort. She returned to her vehicle disappointed, discouraged and upset. Did I mention that Mrs. Taylor was 76 years old?

"The biggest trick the devil played on humanity was convincing them he did not exist."

In other words, if we are unable to identify evil, it will be allowed to continue to operate at a high level. There are family members that do their absolute best to deal with unfair sentencing, cruel mistreatment and rude administration personnel. They send letters, e-mails, cards, photos, funds and unconditional love to the incarcerated, with no guarantee that it will be received. As a prisoner, I often feel powerless when I am forced to watch the stress and depression build up in a mother, father, sister, brother or child for not being able to reach someone they care for deeply, with no ability to change it. I am thankful for all those in my life. Truly, I do not know how you deal with it. #HomeTeam

Not with standing, the FBOP has restrictions on visitors who did not have a prior relationship with the incarcerated person they wish to visit, before incarceration. That is, prisoners are not allowed to congregate with new law-abiding citizens who they have no prior contact with before their conviction. Nope! It's just you and your gang banging cellmate. The same one they forced you to become friends with by disconnecting your e-mails, phone use and other outlets to the free world and people that truly want to see you grow in a positive direction. Consequently, inmates are left with their old vices, and the same thinking that caused them to lose their freedom. By blocking us from bonding with positive thinkers, no change can actually be expected. Does this sound like the road to reform? Maybe it's just me and my webster, but I thought reform was: A change, an improvement, to connect, to revise, to renew. But how can, even a part of this definition be reached with the administration discouraging families and support systems, blocking new avenues towards resources and change? I know! We can't.

"Reform isn't in the FBOP best interest."

Meanwhile, there are many institutions that are now providing "visiting programs" that allow complete strangers to visit inmates with little to no family support. Did you catch that? Allow me to simplify: The FBOP puts policies in place that stop prisoners from building new genuine friendships with law abiding citizens, then break their own rules by allowing strangers of their choosing to infiltrate our lives. They discourage family members from visiting, disrupting communication with others, then violate their own "policies" by pushing strangers into our world. Why? Because it's all about control.

The FBOP doesn't care about re-establishing prisoners with their communities, or encouraging family ties. Strong family ties can help change criminal behavior, and if the administration achieved this goal on a mass level, they would be out of a job. Job security. Social acceptance. The truth is, as long as we are in our cells at count time, and breathing, the administrations conscious is clear. More importantly, their jobs are secure. These are the real reasons they block social sites, media outlets, healthy relationships and family support. In fact, it's easy.

All the administration has to do is claim: It's a threat to security. They need not explain nor answer further questions. Five words and they are allowed to continue business as usual. Maybe it is a threat to their security. Job security! The question is, are their actions legal?

The first Amendment states: Congress shall make no law respecting an establishment of religion, or prohibiting the free exercise thereof, or abridging the Freedom of speech, or of the press, or the right of the people peaceably to assemble, and to petition the government for a redress of grievances.

But the FBOP continues to abridge prisoners' free speech and right to the press. In the Western Region alone, prisoners paced in special housing units are not allowed to receive books, newspapers, magazines or even pens. They are only allowed five envelopes a week, which abridges their letter writing to only twenty a month. The administration is bluntly violating the law of the land with no concern for the prisoner's mental health or his family. I personally sat in the special housing unit for over seven months, under the worst conditions, blind to the outside world, politics or popular events. My mail was withheld (still is) from me for months, as I continued to file grievances and complaints. Not knowing at the time, they had sent numerous letters addressed to me, in addition to making phone calls to the warden, asking about my safety. Calls he never returned.

It would seem that, the Bureau of prisons, considers disconnection from one's family to be a fitting punishment. Even throughout a pandemic. The anger, resentment and frustration such actions cause prisoners, along with the psychological side effects are long lasting. Criminals! Not soldiers or experienced litigants, but convicted criminals, who often respond to injustice with aggression. And with no true understanding or concern for the individuals they are hired to reform, the staff member only sees inmates as callous, belligerent ruffians. And the cycle continues. The administration lobbies for more control (and fire power) and tougher sanctions, while throwing rocks to provoke the prison population. Meanwhile, family ties continue to suffer.

"Family!" The word alone is sacred. In everyone's life, there are boundaries that must be respected. Staff members understand that. Violating this "holy ground", prisoners will often act out, which will result in more punishment and new sanctions. E.g.

A prisoner in Ohio awaited his "none contact" window visit, from his eleven-year-old daughter and long-term girlfriend. After an hour, the visitors stepped into the small visiting booth, both with tears in their eyes. When the prisoner asked for the cause of their sorrow, his girlfriend explained the traumatizing event that took place moments earlier. A staff member in the prison lobby ordered the woman and child to perform a strip search before being allowed to see their incarcerated loved one. The eleven-year-old girl was ordered to take her clothes off, bend at the waist and perform a cough and squat. My hand shakes writing this. Not only because I have a daughter, but imagining the fear and embarrassment these citizens went through is simply appalling. Subsequently, the prisoner was taken to solitary confinement for demanding the names of all officers involved. He was punished for being outraged, and not submissive to the power of the administration. What father, mother or guardian would not take issue with such an unspeakable act by a prison staff member? My prayers go out to those who are left with no options when seeking justice.

The illusion of being a family friendly organization, that the FBOP continue to promote is just that, an illusion! In some institutions, prisoners are only allowed fifteen minutes a day to read, and respond to e-mails. This inconsideration has turned the e-mail system into more of a text service, in which family members are trained to only send short notes and brief thoughts. However, the same system allows inmates thirty minutes to e-mail staff members. Clearly you can see which communication is more important to the administration. Some visiting halls are restricted to only four visitors per inmate. Therefore, the prisoner with five children must leave two at home in order to have an adult bring three to visit. I could write another full chapter on the damage their "restrictions" do to a family bond, but somehow I feel you can already imagine it. New friendships are discouraged at all cost. Pen-pal sites are blocked. Commissary prices are jacked up due to the on-going third-party extortion ring that is known as "the inmate trust fund". Victorville Penitentiary once removed all vending machines from the visiting hall in order to disrupt quality visiting and discourage visitors from arriving. Prisoners and loved ones alike were forced to under-go an eight hour fast in order to complete a full visit. Now does this sound at all like "family friendly"? I don't think so.

The FBOP normally allows prisoners 300 minutes a month of controlled phone use. I.E, 20 fifteen-minute calls a month, with 15-90 minutes in between calls (depending on the facility a prisoner is housed in). On average, a prisoner is allowed to "break up" the phone minutes in order to call multiple family members at different times per month. However, twenty phone calls a month has never been enough to maintain a healthy bond with loved ones on the outside. The administration has known this fact for many years. The annual 2.4 billion dollars that the FBOP phone systems squeezes out of the prisoners and their family members has clearly been enough for the administration throughout the years (where does that money go any ways?) So, in March 2020, the director of the FBOP released a memo that awarded the prison population all over the system with 500 minutes a month (200 extra minutes) and free phone calls, to combat the Coronavirus crisis and social distancing procedures. I for one, was very thankful. That is, until reality re-emerged.

The FBOP is only concerned with appearing to be family friendly, firm and fair. Meanwhile, the truth continues to kick prisoners in the face. The director's memo did not help further family communication at all. In fact, it hurt communication worse than ever before. During the Coronavirus pandemic, prisoners were only allowed outside of their cells for one hour a day (much less for some others), Monday through Friday. On Saturdays and Sundays, prisoners remained locked in their assigned cells twenty-four hours a day. And to ensure that inmates could not capitalize on the director's increased phone minute idea, the administration re-set the phone system to only allow one ten-minute call every 90 minutes. Yep! That's one ten-minute call a day for each prisoner. Which equals fifty minutes a week and two hundred a month. In short, they made it impossible to reach 500 minutes a month, making the director's memo, all for show. During one of the most unprecedented times in our nation's history, the FBOP took phone call use and derailed family communication, while deceiving the general public into believing otherwise. Prison is not a nice place to live.

I have found out that not only is prison not a nice place to live, it's the home of manipulation and psychological warfare. Prison officials smile and shake hands with each other, as they continue to torture human lives behind closed cages. Wardens operate more like terrorists within a society of their own making. They punish bad behavior, and penalize good conduct. Prisoners are left scratching their heads, wondering why they are being treated with such indignation. The only consistency is inconsistency. How can one learn to accept responsibility for actions not their own? The FBOP has adopted a procrustean approach that deems all prisoners the same. Everyone must lose family support and communication, no matter the strength of your values, resources or willingness to correspond. The idea of "family" is turned inward, as more prisoners embrace cellmates while being driven away from their hard-to-reach loved ones. And with the ability to destroy family ties, the administration causes the inmate population to become more desperate for acceptance. Acceptance from who? Acceptance from anybody.

CHAPTER 7

CELLMATES AND INFLUENCES

Under the influence of strong feeling, we are easily deceived. The coward, under the influence of fear, and the lover under that of love, have such illusions that the coward owing to a trifling resemblance, thinks he sees an enemy, and the lover his beloved.
  -Aristotle

A case manager once asked," Are you easily influenced by others?" Answering honestly, I responded," Yeah, are we all?" Considering her silent tongue and awkward facial expression, I do not believe she shared my opinions. Staff members, along with the Administration that programs them, continue to advertise educational programs designed to reform prisoners, and help deviate the future commission of crimes. But these advertisements are misleading. The FBOP perpetuates a system of punishment-no-rewards. Their goal is to destroy inmates' sense of self and individualism through such means as: inmate bashing, bullying and social restrictions. The mental bruises from these actions are often more harmful than the physical abuse performed beyond the cameras' reach. And our brains do not register much difference between physical pain and psychological pain. Abuse is abuse. Prison officials have no real intentions on rehabilitating offenders (that would be bad for business), that job has long been abandoned. Their actions speak louder than policy, but before I illustrate this point, I believe it's important that we take a look at "influence" and what it truly means.

Influence = power, authority or control. The gradual or unseen operation of some cause. To act upon, to persuade.

Now how many times have we allowed a new commercial to hijack our thoughts and desires? Before we can even question the source of our new craving, we are in line at Popeye's Chicken, eager to taste some new concoction filled with delicious fatties. And, even though you have plenty of food in your refrigerator, somehow, your irresponsible spending feels good (and tastes good). That's the power of control. How about the high school kid, who is passionate about a pro career in the NBA, but after speaking with his favorite teacher, is convinced to pursue a life in the armed forces? Is that not the power of authority?

Let us consider your favorite football team, and the sense of pride you may feel after defeating your biggest rivals. That feeling of belonging, the us VS them, the hand slaps and chest bumps, that is the gradual or unseen operation of cause forming inside of you, and you act upon that cause when you buy team jerseys and foam fingers. You are persuaded to watch the outcome of each game, or at least inquire about it. Yeah, I would say we are all easily influenced by others. Wouldn't you?

Influence is the reason women wear makeup and high heels. It's the cause for men shaving their heads and trimming our beards. Vanity movements have influenced us to whiten our teeth and surgically reconstruct our bodies. Billboards tell us to have a snicker. Sneaker ads tell us to just do it. Meanwhile, there are billions of minds lost in the internet, paying attention to other people's lives while not having a true understanding of what they want out of life.

Similarly so, the prison system is designed to influence the prisoners confined, stripping them of individuality and self-respect. The administration wants us all to fit inside a classification folder (The Procrustean approach) as they scheme to achieve more control. But if we (prisoners) are not being influenced toward rehabilitation, or a successful life after prison, then who or what are we being persuaded to become? Let's talk about it.

The federal bureau of prisons force inmates to become cellmates. This "order" is said to promote sociability and companionship. It doesn't! what it does promote is, gang membership, violent clashes and criminal thinking that transforms into future indictments. By forcing a passive, first time offender to live with a criminal idealist, the Administration is systematically creating new crimes. Prisoners are not forced to have cellmates in order to build healthy bonds. We are forced to accept other prisoners in our personal surroundings for two reasons.: The administration wants prisoners to take responsibility for each other's action, and the lack of concern for prisoner safety helps combat issues caused by staff shortage. Therefore, they rely on prisoners to watch prisoners, or face punishment. And with unchecked mental illnesses running wild, this is a job none of us are prepared for.

Remember Tayvon? After his death, his cellmate spent over a year in the special housing unit. Even though the Administration knew the cause of Tayvon's death, alone with his mental health history, his cellmate was made to suffer in the aftermath. It wasn't Tayvon's cellmate's job to keep him alive. Although, he did save Tayvon's life numerous times before, on that fateful night, he returned to the cell after a twelve-hour shift in the mess hall and soon fell into a deep sleep. When he awoke, Tayvon was already deceased. Can you imagine the psychological ramifications, along with the self-blaming and stress Tayvon's cellmate felt? It was staff members job to make sure Tayvon took his pills, not his cellmate's. It was staff members job to keep Tayvon alive, not his cellmates. However, that responsibility has long been passed to the prisoners, who are forced to influence each other, for good or bad. Meanwhile, the Administration continues to create conflict, and punish the prison population for falling victim to the plot.

The FBOP is racially segregated in ways that would make Jim Crow look like the age of Harmony. There are: Black T. V.'s, white tables, Mexican cells, Spanish recreation rooms, native yards and islander computers. Also, there are groups within groups. Bloods, crips, GD's, BGF, Dc Boys, dirty south, Tri-state and 5%er's. when you arrive at any given facility, staff members will ask: "who do you run with?" and if your preferred crew happens to not exist on that particular compound, you are forced to become cellmates with a new influence.

Beyond the physical violence these actions by staff members cause, forcing another man into a stranger's space is often intimidating and awkward. Imagine the government forcing you to live in another man's apartment. How many problems would that bring? "Did you touch my tooth brush?" But the Administration is not concerned about prisoner's safety, only building security. They do not care about our vulnerability, only consolidation. And they could care less about the created tension and ill feelings building up between two strangers locked in a small space no bigger than a closet. And with the majority of today's inmates suffering from some form of mental decline, I find it hard to understand how either offender could possibly be considered safe in their own surrounding. Prisoners suffer from: Depression, anxiety attacks, panic attacks and stress, with no true help available, or an outlet to relieve tension. They often channel their frustration in the wrong direction, and cellmates are forced to become doctors, lawyers and psychiatrists. We are told to practice patience while dealing with the evasion of privacy, corruption of independent thought, friendly extorsion, rude and loud behavior, along with complete ignorance. Once again, prisoners are told they have no right to self-defense. Therefore, any physical altercations arising from these "forced pairing" will equal more punishment for the convicted.

"Show me your friends, and I will tell you who you are."

On federal probation, ex-offenders are not allowed to associate with known felons. Which means, the FBOP policy of forcing prisoners to become social builders and working companions is clearly a set up for failure. Even if cellmates become best of friends, they are not allowed to continue their friendship beyond the prison walls. So why are we being forced to become chummy? Moreover, after spending years living in the same confined space, it's common to become familiar with names, and addresses of family members and loved ones. Is this safe for prisoners? Inmates often learn a great deal about each other by becoming cellmates, and often feel compelled to assist each other when needed. Is this safe for the prison? Cellmates share foods (which is a violation), borrow from each other (another violation), and communicate throughout the night (so much for social distancing). Some appear compatible, while others argue and fight. But more importantly, what future relationships are being built behind these walls? Are we creating reformers, or crime partners?

One of the more solid cellmates of the past was a young man from Harlem, New York. He was very motivated to succeed in life, and kept a positive outlook for most of his time inside the system. We formed a brotherhood, but once he was released back into society, he was told not to associate with known felons. That meant me as well. Known felons were all he had known for the previous eight years, but under federal probation rules, he was restricted from contacting, seeking advice or any form of support from those he trusted most. Upon my own release date, I will have to avoid any support from him also. So once again, what type of social building is being accomplished by forcing prisoners to become cellmates?

The wrong influence becomes a hindrance to all those seeking true reform. Some offenders are often pressured to commit new crimes, join gangs and participate in prison politics, or power struggles within the institution. Depression leads to social suicide as prisoners engage in violent acts, unconscious rage, self-mutilation and childish behavior. Maybe this is the influence the Administration wants the prison population to become infected with. Each violent case, cause and clash show that a minor dispute can become a serious issue.

And with nowhere to retreat, in order to clear our heads, cellmates often battle for the right to be themselves. A prisoner's cell should be a safe haven from physical threats, psychological wars, emotional liability and mental confusion. But the dual problems of de-institutionalization and forced pairings continue to cause injustice around every corner. American prisons have become asylums, and prison officials have no concern for the safety of the mentally ill or the practically sane. Prisoners with the right ideas often replace them with survival tactics or enough medication to stop them from thinking at all. *When in Rome, do as the romans do.*

I met a man by the name Doctor Mutula Shakur, who I came to admire very much. His dedication to education amongst constant chaos and confusion was notably impressive. He has spent over 30 years incarcerated with little-to no incident reports on his discipline record. I once asked him: "how could you remain shot (another word for write ups) free for so long?" and he said, "I don't catch shots, shots have to catch me."

The implication was clear. Mr. Shakur didn't receive incident reports, unlike thousands of federal prisoners throughout the system, for one reason above all, he continued to move. Move, as in, being active. His schedule consisted of educational programs designed to help prisoners better themselves, both physically and mentally. When he wasn't teaching a course, he was preparing new curriculums, or exercising his mind by jogging or reading. There are prisoners like Mr. Shakur who continue to fight for their own sanity, within a system built to distract and detach us from reality. Unfortunately, Doctor Mutula Shakur continues to be held unjustly. He is a political prisoner, and there will be no justice for him so long as politicians continue to influence the criminal justice system with deep seeded hatred, and plans for revenge, not rehabilitation.

The Federal Bureau of prisons now enforce policies that punish all occupants of an assigned cell, regardless of who committed the institutional infraction. Let me be clear: if a piece of illegal narcotics is found in one cellmate's bedsheets, staff members are ordered to take both cellmates to the special housing unit. One could scream to the heavens that the contraband found is his, and his cellmate has nothing to do with it. It wouldn't matter. Policy allows staff members to punish both inmates, regardless of who is responsible. Can you imagine the problems those actions by the Administration cause? Not only is it completely unjust to hold me accountable for my cellmate's actions, but it also causes tension between us. Thoughts begin to form in an inmate's mind as he searches for the cause of his discomfort. Placed in a lose-lose situation, a confrontation bound to arise. My cellmate should never be responsible for my action, nor should I for his own. But the FBOP engages in a psychological war that continues to create problems among the prison population at the hands of an indifferent administration, that is paid to ensure the safety of each prisoner.

I was placed in solitary confinement for allegations of drug introduction. When I refused to take responsibility for these false claims, staff member threw my former cellmate in the special housing unit, and threatened to charge him with crimes, unless he agreed to help them find me guilty. They held him for over a year, destroyed communications with his loved ones, wrote frivolous reports against him, transferred him over 3,000 miles away from his release address, fumbled his personal property and pushed his release date backwards. All of this, because he refused to substantiate their false claims against me. *Mack Major # Realone*

It's illegal to force a confession, inside prison and outside. However, the FBOP embraces shady methods behind guarded walls, with no true oversight. A staff member could set a prisoner on fire and be five years retired before the smoke clears. The administrative remedy process is blocked by door keepers. Meanwhile, prisoners are infected, influenced, abused, disrespected, bullied and forced into a slumber. Policies are crafted to subpress (not rehabilitate). Wardens pass down orders to force prisoners to walk and talk and dress alike. The FBOP punishes independent thought. Even the "correctional officers" are not allowed to think. Control, and more control is the chief aim while confused inmates continue to fight each other over trivial issues; and formerly trained soldiers are programmed to carry out orders that push the Administration's agenda. More violence equals more control, and each incident report gains a prisoner more time incarcerated. What a system.

Prisoners are influenced by the convicted felons they live among. Therefore, if we are gone to influence change, speaking out against this systematic indifference is the true "First step". People are influenced by everything around them. A white officer murders and unarmed black man and the stench of injustice effects the whole country. Including the prisoners. The system of corruption is multiplied throughout the hard drive. Meaning that officers are trained to be biased and heartless (or allowed to). They are recruited from the armed service where "no one comes back whole," to inflict pain and punishment without thought or emotion. This is no secret society, or some conspiracy theory with unproven facts driving the narrative. Everything I share with you is on record, and attainable. The question is, do you really want to know? New knowledge brings new responsibility. "The higher ups" won't punish themselves, and BOP staff members are paid salaries they can't afford to lose. Their silence is paid for in American Currency while prisoners continue to suffer. So then, regardless of how uncomfortable it may become, I have no choice but to carry on the conversation. Remedies exhausted. This one is for the people.

In conclusion, inmates should be allowed to cell alone; when requested, and posing no threat to security. There are plenty of empty cells in every institution (sometimes complete cell blocks). Prisoners have a right to be safe from mental threats as well as physical ones. Notwithstanding, a prisoner should be allowed to seek reform, without the influence or interruption of others, who desire less of themselves. Inmates are not doctors. It is not their job to attend to other inmates (unless they are mental health companions), or halt suicide attempts. Forcing prisoners to live with each other puts both men in danger, and clearly shows the lack of concern for safety. Not to forget the mental effects a death in closed quarters can cause the surviving occupant. Ultimately, officers need to be retrained, re-named and supervised by new minded superiors with compassion, for the future of our penal system. We cannot continue to numb the minds of our convicted with pills and pamphlets, then expect to see change. It doesn't work that way. If the Coronavirus pandemic taught us anything, it should be the fact that no one is immune to indifference. One way or the other, it soon affects us all.

CHAPTER 8

THE CORONAVIRUS

At the time of my removal afromt the special housing at Victorville USP, the first positive Coronavirus case in the building had been confirmed. And although I showed no signs of the virus, I was ordered to be relocated inside "quarantine unit". Staff members in paper gowns escorted me to a secured location to perform a covid-19 test. It would be the first of over a dozen similar test, in which staff members refused to provide me the results. I would learn later, the six-step process that determined a positive or negative reading:

Known as the gold standard lab test for covid-19, PCR's procedure accurate results, but labs can process one a limited number of their tests, which also require chemical supplies and enough trained lab workers. How the process works: First the inmate is swabbed deep in the nose. Secondly, the swab is put in a tube, broken off and sealed. Next, the sample is sent to a lab to be analyzed, and this could take several days. In the lab, a technician adds primers and nucleotides to the sample. These primers bind to the ribonucleic acid (RNA) of the virus. The nucleotides reproduce the virus' genetic material. Then the sample is added to a polymerase chain reaction (PCR) machine that heats and cools, causing the cirrus RNA to split and bind the nucleotides multiplying in the process. Finally, the cirrus RNA, multiplied millions of times, makes it easier to identify. The data is plotted on a curve, and from that curve, results are determined.

Results that the inmate has no right to examine. The administration continued to keep a blindfold over our eyes, not only concerning our own health, but also the number of staff members infected with the deadly virus. In June, 2020, the FBOP decided it would be a good idea to continue business as usual, by transferring prisoners in and out the facility during the worst pandemic in modern history. Even after our country wide orders to remain indoors. After the painful process of being tested, I was escorted to a quarantine unit that, at that time had zero confirmed cases of covid-19. We were not allowed phone calls, e-mails, visit or commissary. It would seem that, the so called "quarantine unit" was being used to fulfill transfer orders, not to prevent the spread of a virus none of us had at the time, but that fact would soon change. The Administration shuffled inmates in and out for over seven months, giving each prisoner a chance to be exposed to new carriers of the Coronavirus. I often wondered why staff members would continue such dangerous practice, and had to remind myself: The officers are here to protect the building, not the prisoners inside it. Besides, there were more severe cases all over the system that would raise eyebrows, as well as lit candles.

The Coronavirus spread like a rumor in the night. Before the sun came up, it had left China (the said origin of the virus), infected numerous countries and crossed the ocean, headed for the United States. In early March 2020, news headlines warned prison officials that jails would be a potential hot bed for covid-19, the disease caused by the novel Coronavirus. They were ordered to step up inmate screenings, sanitizing jail cells and to urge lawyers to scale back in person visits to prevent the new Coronavirus from spreading through their vast inmate populations.

"Jail operators in the U.S. are coming to the growing realization that it's only a matter of time before it strikes."

"Jails are, you know, just prime opportunities for something like this to spread," said Bossner Parish Shariff Julian Whittington, the president of the Louisiana sheriff's association. "I'm a realist and I suspect more than likely, sometime it's going to pop up in somebody's jail."

On March 12th, the FBOP temporarily suspended visits from family and friends at each one of its facilities around the country- Health officials have been warning for more than a decade about the dangers of outbreaks in jails and prisons, which are ideal environments for virus outbreaks: Inmates share small cells with total strangers, use toilets just a few feet from their beds, and are herded into day rooms where they spend hours at a time together. Practicing even the simplest hygiene, such as washing hands, is not a given in such environments. Hand sanitizer is often treated as contraband because it contains alcohol. Inmates go in groups to court, where they wait together in cramped holding areas. San Antonio based attorney Joseph Hoelscher said several judges have encouraged attorneys to post-pone routine courthouse appearances for cases that are not nearing trial, to avoid having to bring prisoners to the courthouse.

"We are not going to any jails," he said. "That would be the first population where it would spread. And they would get the worst medical care."

After the swine flu outbreak in 2009, which infected hundreds of prisoners across the country, most prison systems created pandemic preparation plans. The FBOP instituted a new screening tool that includes questions about whether inmates or staff members have traveled through any risk countries, had close contact with anyone diagnosed with covid-19 or been deployed to areas with the virus within two weeks. The tool, obtained by the associated press, also looks to assess possible symptoms, including fever, cough and shortness of breath.

In New York city, the Department of corrections cleaned and sanitized cells, common spaces, showers and transport buses. Anyone sick at Rikers Island, the notorious New York City Jail, where Harvey Weinstein was held, was screened for potential trips to an area hospital or the department's communicable disease unit.

In Miami, "any newly arrested persons suspected of having the virus will be diverted to a hospital," said corrections and rehabilitation department spokeswoman Dominique Moody. She said," The department has also secured space for a medical quarantine for any of the 3,900 inmates already in custody, if it becomes necessary."

"Prison staff are being trained in many facilities on how to recognize symptoms and are being given supplies for protection, such as masks, gloves and eye protection. Meanwhile, officials are working to secure more money to cover cost of employees, including jail guards need to stay home sick."

U.S. District court Judge Collen McMahon quietly ordered all inmates at the nearby federal jail to be screened for fevers, and said they should not appear in court if they have a temperature of 100.4 degrees Fahrenheit or higher.

With all these precautions all these warnings, how is it that, the numbers inside American prisons continued to rise? On April 28th, 2020, the USA Today reported: The Federal Bureau of Prisons, the largest detention system in the country, has announced that it too is expanding testing for asymptomatic inmates in an attempt to control the spread of the virus, that has so far infected nearly 1,000 inmate and staff workers, the numbers morphed into 2,818 prisoners and 262 staff members, with over 50 inmate deaths.

"Across the country, Federal prisons have become a hotbed for Coronavirus infections. Hundreds of prisoners and several dozen prison staff have died," according to the American civil liberties union.

We were told it was coming, we were warned about the impossible task of practicing social distancing while the FBOP still forces inmates to cell together, even though there are plenty of empty cells. Family and attorney visits were suspended in order to help stop the spread. Prison staff members were "trained" to recognize symptoms. Inmates were screened and quarantined. Cells, common spaces, showers and transportation buses were cleaned and sanitized. Yet and still, over 50 deaths in under 60 days. What happened? Indifference, neglect, abuse of authority, inmate bullying and the lack of compassion for human lives.

The inmate population did not receive face masks until May 2020. Staff members were not "ordered" to wear face masks until June 2020. Correctional officers were heard claiming proudly: It's a personal choice. Referring to their use of protection. For the prisoners, there was only one sure way of contracting covid-19, the disease caused by the novel Coronavirus. We had no choice. It could only come from one source. The men and women coughing into the open air as they performed cell extractions, brushing off the seriousness of a deadly virus sweeping the nation, lacking concern for the prisoners they were hired to protect. One source! Staff. And as words like "quarantine" became most popular in the common syntax, the Bureau of prisons used every opportunity to further subpress the inmate population.

"Federal courts have an obligation to ensure that prisons are not deliberately indifferent in the face of danger and death." -Sonia Sotomayor

Sorry Miss Sotomayor, but the courts play on the same team that carried the virus into Federal facilities, and infected thousands of the inmate population. At Lompoc USP, prisoners complained about the dangerous living spaces that won't allow two men to walk the cell floor at the same time. The Administration refused to allow inmate to purchase soap, while only providing small portions of hygiene products per week. So small in fact, prisoners had to choose between taking showers regularly or washing their hands daily. Correctional officers are taught to dismiss complaints from inmates while prescribing more control to every situation. And with over 240 inmates consolidated on top of each other, with open bar cells and only one exit, I can safely say that the Administration at Lompoc USP have been deliberately indifferent in the face of danger and death long before the Coronavirus attacked our "normal" way of everyday life. I mean, I should know right, I was there.

On May 9th, 2020, Richard Winton reported: The number of inmates infected with the Coronavirus at a Federal prison in Lompoc, California shot up to 792 this week, making it the largest Federal penitentiary outbreak in the nation, surpassing a facility on Terminal Island in San Pedro, where 644 inmates have contracted the virus. Nearly, 70% of the inmates at Lompoc have tested positive, exploding by more than 300 in recent days, officials reported. Lompoc along with Terminal Island accounted for over 47% of all Federal inmates who tested positive nationwide. Both prisons over went widespread testing of hundreds of inmates, even without symptoms.

At that time, only eleven staff members were reported to have been infected at the Lompoc facility, which houses 1,162 low-security inmates. A military mobile hospital was built on the grounds to cope with the growing numbers of stricken patients. At the neighboring medium-security prison on the same grounds, 31 inmates died from contracting the virus in the dangerous closed setting. Combined, the two Federal prisons in Lompoc had over 825 infected inmates, according to the Federal Bureau of prisons.

Look at those numbers again. Over 825 inmates infected, and roughly 22 staff members. How is that possibly? As I stated before, there were over 240 prisoners consolidated on top of each other in every cell block. Even though with numerous completely empty cells, the administration continued to force prisoners to live together inside of rooms no bigger than a broom closet, during a global pandemic, solely for staff convenience. You would think the Administration at Lompoc would have learned a lesson after the mumps outbreak covered the building in September-December 2019. But the FBOP has a long history of placing inmates in harm's way, not protecting them from it. During the mumps outbreak, Lompoc officials banded the prison population in special housing units from ordering soap and hygiene products. Soap! The chemical used to fight germs and deadly infections. Staff members are hired to protect the building, not the persons housed inside them. The message is, inmates do not matter.

Santa Barbara County Supervisor, Gregg Hart can tell you that. He said, "The prison numbers are making it hard for the county to meet Governor Gavin Newson's new requirements for more wide-spread re-opening around the state".

Forget the fact that human beings are dying prematurely, his concerns are about re-opening the county. Business as usual. Meanwhile, one man died within days of his release date. Efrem Stutson, a 60-year-old man released from Lompoc after serving 27 years for selling cocaine. Within hours of getting off the bus in San Bernardino, he was hospitalized. Five days later he was pronounced dead after contracting covid-19. His sister stated that he became sick as he was about to be released and was hardly able to walk off the bus.

On April 1st, 2020, the FBOP implemented a strict policy of keeping inmates in their assigned quarters for 14 days and barring all transfers. And with over 14,000 inmates held in federal prisons and other facilities, it was reported that 3,082 inmates and 248 staff members over all had tested positive for the Coronavirus nationwide. However, as the Administration continued to manipulate the true numbers of the infected, positive cases continued to rise.

Assemblyman Jordan Cunningham along with some Northern Santa Barbara County leaders called on the California Department of Public Health to exclude the covid-19 positive case count at Lompoc prison complex from Santa Barbara County numbers. Still, more concerned with re-opening then the safety of the lives suffering inside the prison complex.

Cunningham stated, "The outbreak only occurred at this magnitude because the FBOP's failure to act in a timely manner".

According to reports in the Washington Post, it took the FBOP until April 1st to start enacting social distancing measures among inmates. Local officials request for more information were denied, and the FBOP through the justice department requested not to publicize the number of hospitalized inmates, and where those inmates were being treated.

This much is true. But the "Social distancing" measures enacted, forced prisoners to remain in cells with other prisoners while numerous cells remained empty. To state the least, one major problem with this tactic is, I can only be responsible for the washing of my own hands, and safeguarding myself against infection, while my cellmate doesn't care, and doesn't believe in practicing good hygiene with the virus on the loose or without it. Thus, we potentially lose two lives while failing to protect one. Why? Because staff members are invested in making their shift easier, not providing inmates with the proper protection needed. Even when "ordered" to, the Administration always finds a loophole to circumvent fairness, and carry out directives as they see fit. Hence the "free" 300-minute phone calls that no inmate was allowed to explore completely. Simply said, the FBOP is not in business to save lives, only to confine them.

Attorney, Bob Sanger of Santa Barbara County got it right, "There are conditions there that are very troubling. People should not be subjected to that, no matter what they're sentenced for. In my opinion, it's unconstitutional. People in many cases, having to sleep on the floor or confined to facilities for far fewer people. Inmates at Lompoc Federal prison are serving a variety of sentences. People are being confined to places that threaten their lives. And some are dying. They weren't sentenced to death. They were sentenced there for a period of years, and they have people that love them."

By May 9th, 2020, two inmates died of the covid-19, 905 inmates tested positive, and 34 staff members had contracted the disease at Lompoc Federal Correction Complex alone. On April 3rd, U.S. Attorney General William Barr wrote a memo to the director of the Bureau of Prisons, ordering supervised release or transfers for inmates in facilities with outbreaks.

"For all inmates you deem suitable candidates for home confinement, you are directed to immediately process them for transfer and then immediately transfer them following a 14-day quarantine at an appropriate

BOP facility, or in appropriate cases, subject to your case-by-case discretion, in the residence to which the inmate is being transferred,"

-Attorney General, William Barr.

Mr. Barr soon after became under fire for the FBOP staff members not acting fast enough to transfer or release "suitable" inmates. But the Administration are masters at utilizing word play to their own advantage. The key words in William Barr's directive were: Deem suitable. These words gave the Administration all the time they wish to drag their feet while lives were at stake. *Case-by case discretion.*

Interestingly so, on March 11th,2020, news headlines read: Earlier this week in Iran, 54,000 inmates were temporarily released back into the country amid virus fears. Iran has a population of 65,875,223 million people, and in early March they released 54,000 inmates amid the virus scares. In contrast, America, home of 2million prisoners, released only 1,290 inmates by late April 2020. America's 2million prison population is more than 15 states in our country. Out of the 187,00 Federal prisoners, 20,000 are over the age of 56. Prison officials stated that the elderly would be their primary concern, with early release or home confinement. But only 1,280 inmates were transferred by late April 2020.

Let's be clear. Although I am not among the elderly, or high-risk prisoners, it means something to see your country's justice system acting fairly in the midst of a global pandemic. Unfortunately, the FBOP received the memo but chose to interpret it as they saw fit. So as suitable subjects were considered, at least one inmate took matters into his own hands.

Early in the month of May, an inmate escaped from a prison camp at Butner in North Carolina, saying later that he had feared contracting the Coronavirus. Other prisoners like Barry Taylor tried to take the legal path by requestion a transfer to home confinement. Barry, who was 68, shared a 70-square-foot living space with two other inmates and 16 toilets with about 150 people in the Federal prison. That's how he described his living quarters at Butner Federal Correctional Complex in a phone interview with the News and observer. He explained he had open heart surgery two years ago, leaving him vulnerable to the virus that killed five inmates at Butner, at the time. In a setting where social distancing is very difficult, the Bureau had 65 inmates and 27 staff members test positive for covid-19 at Butner facilities. The number would later rise as prison officials neglected to follow Attorney general Barr's orders.

Some who had saw the pandemic's effects on Butner, firsthand, said more should have been done. KC Gleaton was released from Butner on April 9th as scheduled, he served 16 months in a plea deal for wire fraud conspiracy. He was not part of the transfers to home confinement. He later said that other inmates along with himself had been kept in closed quarters without the social distancing of 6 feet of separation, required in Governor Ray Cooper's statewide stay at home orders, to control the spread of the pandemic.

"There's no way to do that, it's just impossible for that to happen," he said. "People were scared for their lives."

Geaton said the prisoner who escaped from Butner fled because of the Coronavirus pandemic. Something that escapee Richard R. Cephas confirmed in an interview with the news and observer while on the run: "He left because he was afraid, he was going to be left with a death sentence", said Gleaton. "I felt the same way, but lucky enough, I was getting out in a few days. Believe me, I asked if I could be let out early. Inmates have contact with prison staff when they eat, discuss their cases, go into recreation yards, to the library and when correctional officers check on them multiple times throughout the day. Lives are at risk. The most important thing, and very first thing is to get those people out of there. People in there with none-violent felonies, left to die. That's not the way it should be"

And he's right! It shouldn't be that way. But the Administration continued to drag their feet as they decided who to "deem" proper for home confinement.

Barry Taylor said, "Until two weeks ago, there wasn't enough soap in the dispensers. I do not wish to die in the BOP from Coronavirus."

Taylor hoped to be one of the chosen inmates transferred to home confinement. He felt he should have been released because of his age, medical records, conviction for a none-violent offense and his facility's status as low-level security (all requirements for home confinement transfers listed in William Barr's directives). But his request remained in limbo along with thousands seeking home placings as the news headlines continued to roll.

Posted on April 17th, 2020: Authorities said Friday that another inmate has died from covid-19 at a Federal prison near Butner. The latest death brings the total at the prison complex to at least five. The Federal Bureau of Prisons reported that there are at least 91 covid-19 cases at the prison, including staff and inmates. Just Wednesday, there were 80 cases, officials said, Fabian Tinsley, 67 who was serving a 23-year sentence from crimes in Washington D.C. died Thursday. Tinsley was first taken to a nearby hospital on April 6th. Tinsley had long term, pre-existing medical conditions which the CDC lists as risk factors for developing more severe covid-19 cases.

The first confirmed covid-19 death of a federal inmate took place March 28th, at a prison in Oakdale Louisiana. The man's name was Patrick Jones. On a Friday, six more had died. On March 24th, inmate Michael Lilley, who was 55 years old, went into respiratory failure at the facility. While at the hospital, Lilley tested positive for covid-19. His condition later declined, and he was placed on a ventilator. On April 15th, Lilley was pronounced dead. He had a long term pre-existing medical condition that the CDC listed as a factor for developing a more severe covid-19 case. George Jeffus, who was 76 years old, was transported to a local hospital on April 3rd after going into respiratory failure at Oakdale. Jeffus tested positive for covid-19 while at the hospital and was placed on a ventilator when his condition worsened. On April 7th, the ventilator was replaced with a high-flow oxygen mask, and Jeffus showed no signs of improvement. Jeffus had long-term pre-existing medical conditions. On April 9th, he died of the disease caused by the Coronavirus.

These are some of the lives lost due to the indifference, and neglect from the FBOP. Think not? Examine this: We did not receive face masks (the prisoners) until late April, early May 2020. Even then, prisoners were not ordered to wear them until weeks later, while staff members considered their own use of similar face covering to be a "personal choice". Meanwhile, the death toll continued to mount.

On March 26th, Wallace Holley Jr was transported to a local hospital after going into respiratory failure at FCI Oakdale. While at the hospital, Holley tested positive for covid-19 and was placed on a ventilator when his condition worsened. Holley had long term pre-existing medical conditions. He died of the disease on April 2nd. Prisoners in the minimum-security camp watched anxiously as ambulances came and went. They listened into the chatter on guard's radios about the Coronavirus outbreak among staff and inmates in the building, and they started to become concerned. The reports of death spread and fear at the camp intensified.

"As of now, it's like we are on death row, just waiting to catch the virus," one prisoner at the camp wrote.

The ACLU filed a class action lawsuit that sought to get medically vulnerable prisoners released from Oakdale. The suit defined "medically-vulnerable" as any person over the age of 50, along with anyone with a host of pre-existing medical conditions such as moderate to severe asthma, diabetes, or conditions that could cause them to become immuno-compromised, such as cancer treatment. It named the warden of the prison, Rodney Myers, and the Director of the BOP, Michael Carvajal, as defendants. The lawsuit established that there were 748 prisoners at FCC Oakdale that are medically vulnerable, and that being held at Oakdale, violates the Eighth Amendment's prohibition on cruel and unusual punishment.

In the memo, Barr gave the BOP authority to release inmates without electronic monitoring, due to the limited resources at the agency and the U.S. Probation office.

"Given the speed which this disease has spread through the general public, it is clear that time is of the essence," Barr wrote. "Please implement this memorandum as quickly as possible and keep me closely apprised of your progress."

The problem was, Barr gave the BOP "authority". He did not order them to do it. In turn, he dusted off his hands and left matters to the same jailers conditioned to mistreat the inmate. BOP officials never responded to questions about their progress in implementing Barr's directive at FCC Oakdale specifically, but in a statement, a Bureau spokesperson said that since March 26th, the BOP has placed "an additional 615 inmates on home confinement."

Iran released 54,000 inmates in early March. With deaths caused by the virus mounting up, why would the United States move so slowly to protect the lives of the incarcerated? Oakdale was particularly struck hard by the Coronavirus outbreak, along with Lompoc, Terminal Island and Butner. Yet and still, any real actions to prevent the spread, on behalf of the FBOP came very slowly, if at all. It would seem, only those on their death bed were "deemed suitable". And even then, The Administration acted less from compassion, and more in the interest of cost effectiveness, in order to skip out on the funeral cost, by allowing ex-offenders to die at home. The headlines read: Oakdale inmate dies from covid-19, two days after scheduled release."

On Wednesday, April 15th, 2020, inmate George Escamilla went into respiratory failure at the Satellite Prison Camp (SPC) in Oakdale, Louisiana. He was evaluated by institutional medical staff and transported to a local hospital for further treatment and evaluation. While in the hospital, Escamilla tested positive for covid-19. On Thursday April 30th, 2020, his condition declined, and he was placed on a ventilator. On Friday, May 8th, 2020, Escamilla, who had long term, pre-existing medical conditions, which the CDC listed as risk factors for developing more severe covid-19 disease, was pronounced dead by hospital staff.

Escamilla was a 67-year-old man, who was sentenced for possession with intent to distribute 5 kilograms of cocaine and Aiding and Abetting charges. Arrangements began back in mid-March for George to be released from the Federal prison in Oakdale, Louisiana to home confinement. Instead, on May 8th, two days after his scheduled release date, he became another victim to covid-19 and the FBOP's negligence to act.

Escamilla was the eighth prisoner to die from the disease at Oakdale. At the time of his death, he was nearly 12 years into a 16-year sentence. The Federal Bureau of Prisons was said to have "prioritized" his release, particularly because he was vulnerable to complications from the disease. Escamilla was wheelchair bound, having lost both legs as a result of complications from diabetes (a major underlying risk factor for covid-19). He was also a father and a grandfather. His imminent release was eagerly anticipated by those close to him.

"He was someone that whenever he called and I had a problem, I knew I could talk to him about things that I couldn't talk to my parents about," his grand-daughter, Frida Escamilla said.

His death illustrated the failures of the Federal prison system to properly respond to the pandemic with compassion rather than castigation. Public health experts warned that prisons and jails were uniquely susceptible to the spread of the virus, due to the inability for prisoners to practice social distancing, and in many cases (like Lompoc), the lack of hygiene products available. On March 18th, Escamilla was given a release date on home confinement, of May 6th. Prior to that, he was supposed to spend two weeks in quarantine at the prison. The Coronavirus outbreak at Federal Correction Complex Oakdale was serious. Escamilla's death was avoidable, if not for William Barr's congenial memo, and the FBOP's nonchalant response. By April 7th, five prisoners at FCI Oakdale had already died, and here was a man waiting almost two months to be released. Escamilla was one of about 140 prisoners being held at the camp, all living a dorm-style setting, with bunkbeds almost three feet apart.

But despite the proven threat of the virus, Escamilla's high-risk factors, and the fact that he appeared to have already been cleared for home confinement, he was not immediately transferred. In fact, he remained in the minimum-security prison camp until April 15th, when he developed respiratory failure and was taken to a local hospital where he tested positive for covid-19. It wasn't until April 30th, over two weeks after his hospitalization, when his condition declined that the prison contacted his son to inform him that Escamilla had tested positive.

"Then they called again." said his son George Jr.

"They told us that his kidney was not reacting to the medicine."

Instead of George Jr picking up his father and bringing him back home, to re-unite with his family, he drove to Alexandria Hospital with his wife to claim his father's body.

"I can't understand it. I am holding the people at FCI Oakdale accountable." George Escamilla Jr declared.

And he should hold them accountable. We all should. There are many inmates such as Escamilla who cannot even get out of the bed without the help of a fellow prisoner. At Lompoc, I personally witnessed a prisoner wheelchair bound, lower half of his body missing, struggling to maintain a daily life with only the compassion of convicted felons to look forward to. These are vulnerable, non-violent offenders who are being left to die in a system that only values complete control.

On May 16th, 2020, the Federal Bureau of Prisons announced it would begin moving about 6,800 inmates who had been waiting in local detention centers across the U.S. "It's not clear when it will begin, but the inmates will be sent to one of three designated quarantine sites, FCC Yazoo city, FCC Victorville in California and FTC Oklahoma City, or to a Bureau of Prisons detention Center". But why? Why shuffle prisoners around in the middle of a global pandemic? Wouldn't it have been safer to remain still, allowing the virus to pass? As the country began talks about "opening up", the Federal prison system continued its ban on visitors and full operations. But not transfers.

The Bureau announced that the Warden at Louisiana Federal Prison Complex, where eight inmates had died of the Coronavirus had been put on a "temporary duty assignment" at a regional office. As the Warden at Oakdale, Rodney Myers faced criticism from employees for testing shortages and a lack of transparency on which inmates, and how many had tested positive.

Transparency. That's a nice word. Meaning: Readily understood, or clear. Which brings me to my next point. Staff members don't have to stand silent as injustice is carried out right in front of them. The convicted are already being punished, that's what the sentence was for. If you continue to allow physical, as well as mental abuse, along with neglect and indifference then you are equally as guilty as a Warden unconcerned with the safety of the prisoners he was hired to protect. The Coronavirus killed millions across the world and infected our lives forever. But what do you do when lives are at stake? Do you act, or do you wait for others to act out? In the prison system, oftentimes, true pain is hard to see. But do I honestly have to be dying in order to be treated as a human being?

I was placed on a quarantine unit, where no one tested positive for the virus, for months. We were under fed and not allowed to contact our families through e-mail, phones or visits. The Warden issued five mailing envelopes and five stamps per month. We were only allowed out of our cells to take showers three times a week. These harsh conditions continued until I was transferred to the ADX complex in Florence Colorado. Florence had their own routine, which included, allowing newly transferred inmates to mingle with the established population. There were no regular temperature checks, nor covid-19 testing. The staff at Florence "claimed" to be concerned about the safety of the inmate population. But once again, their actions belied their words. New arrivals were placed on units with the general population, and allowed to use the same e-mail system, phone system and showers. This consistent blending put inmates at a higher risk to contract the deadly virus. New inmates meant new chances to cause a spread.

On February 5th, 2021, after almost a complete year of unprecedented suffering, delays and unnecessary movements due to The Administration's neglect and indifference, the inevitable happened. The entire unit in which I was assigned to, contracted the Coronavirus, including myself.

CHAPTER 9

INMATES AND CONVICTS

"He is taught to love the Devil."
"Why does he love the Devil?"
"Because the Devil gives him nothing."
-Muhammad

During World War II, Nazi soldiers imprisoned Jewish Men inside what was called: Concentration Camps. These men were forced to work under unspeakable conditions while awaiting their own deaths. Prisoners fought among each other over trivial issues such as extra bread and better boots. If a prisoner felt sick or became too weak to work, he would be executed at once. Suffering became a way of life for these imprisoned men. Consequently, the violent acts towards each other grew. The Jewish prisoners who found favor with the guards (by informing on fellow prisoners) were treated slightly better than others, and although death was certain to all, these prisoners worked hard to make their captors smile. It would seem that, an increased level of discomfort and punishment can motivate its target to comply or submit. Moreover, a continued struggle, both mentally and physically will force the oppressed to even oppress themselves.

From January 2016 until September of the same year, the Warden, along with his captain and staff members put a plan in motion to disrupt the prison population at Victorville USP. The Warden ordered institutional lock downs, every week over minor disputes to raise tension and frustration among the incarcerated. Visits were terminated without cause, and family communication were cut off. Inmate on inmate altercations increased, as the Warden used bad behavior to justify new sanctions, he later introduced. The "lock downs" continued and inmates began pointing fingers at each other over the unfair treatment they were all receiving. Every week brought more discipline for actions unknown to most of the prison population.

The Warden snatched away: Store spending limits, reading books, recreation time, visit points and institutional programing in order to "stir things up". Prisoners filed numerous complaints to address the unfair treatment, and robbery of earned privileges. All to no avail. The Administration simply slammed its iron fist on the table to further demonstrate its supreme powers. Confused and angry, inmates turned their aggression inward, as punishment came from all angles. In May 2016 a large race riot erupted throughout the complex. Inmates and staff members suffered many injuries. Ambulance workers pushed stretchers in and out of the building for hours. Staff members supplied cases of water to help hydrate their workers. The prison was placed on permanent lock down throughout the summer, as the Administration continued to use psychological warfare against the incarcerated. The Warden used the extended lock down period to construct a brick wall inside the dining hall. He would claim, the wall was built to protect others from future attacks, when in fact, it was his own actions that caused the increase of violence at the institution.

After the wall was built, and the prison forever changed, the Warden relocated, leaving behind a short legacy of provoked violence and justified discipline. But let's not give him all the blame. The FBOP has long used prisoners for social behavior experiments. E.g., James "Whitey" Bulgar received a sentence reduction for becoming a government guineapig in LSD testing. The Administration wanted to study how the drug affected the human brain. Two dozen murders later, I guess they found out.

I have spent a lot of time and thought detailing the cruel and unfair actions of the prison Administration, their staff members and those hired to reform the prisoner. However, as adults, we must be aware of our own actions and the part we play in our own self destruction. Who do you think built that wall in the dining hall? As prisoners, we are sentenced to serve time for crimes committed. As prisoners, we have many inalienable rights. As prisoners, we are not slaves! Slavery was a form of incarceration that dehumanized its victims as much by denying them responsibility for their lives as well as providing them with a subsistence existence by denying them freedom. The thirteenth Amendment says: Neither slavery nor involuntary servitude, except as a punishment for a crime where of the party shall have been duly convicted, shall exist within the United States, or any place subject to their jurisdiction. But inmates often try to justify their own ignorance. The abused minds of the oppressed often except servitude as obligations for being caught. When in fact, "except as a punishment for crimes" means that, American citizens can be sentenced to serve duties such as community service. While most convicted felons of today are sentenced to serve "time", as manual duty or involuntary servitude. So again, I ask, who built that wall?

According to webster, an "inmate" is a resident of a mental institution or asylum. Albeit I agree, the definition has been expanded to include prisoners, and within the prison system, the title continues to be used to belittle and dehumanize. Prison officials look down on inmates like a piece of used gum infecting the prison tiles. They are careful not to step directly on them, while avoiding contact daily. By side stepping their existence, staff members promote indifference, and cause inmates to wonder if they exist at all. While some inmates seek out their oppressor's approval, hoping for acceptance and advice; others hustle and bustle for pennies on a dollar, and left-over scrapes. Let's be clear, I'm not advocating a work stoppage, or insolent behavior. I completely understand that many prisoners depend on the money they receive from work detail within the institution, and a diligent work ethic is always admirable. But so is self-respect. Does an inmate have the right to be treated fairly? Or is it part of his punishment, for being duly convicted to receive a physical and psychological smack down along with the incarcerated period?

I digressed. We need to take responsibility here. After all, who can complain about the conditions of life without taking steps to improve that same life? Politicians, activists and celebrities can speak out against inmate bashing, and government policies that continue to subpress the incarcerated, but if we, the incarcerated, choose to do nothing about our own circumstances, then what's the point? Prison guards, along with the Administration they work for often treat inmates poorly. Facts! But how do inmates treat themselves?

"I never had a father to show me how to be a man."

"My mother was never there for me."

"Nobody is looking out for me."

I feel you! Unconsciously, I have borrowed some of these self-defeating statements myself. But often, when you are forced to spend months that turn into years inside a small cell somewhere, lost in the system, you start to realize the truth. It's all on you! It doesn't matter who did it, or how it got done. How you respond is completely up to you. If you want others to respect you, first you must respect yourself. Even then, you may not receive the respect you feel you deserve, but no one cares. How you deal with the fact will make you or brake you. Fight or flight, accept or reject, but self-respect is choice. You either have it or you don't.

Psychosexual inmates expose their private parts to female officers, and when they receive incident reports, they lose face and good time credits. That's not player. Inmates search the yard for used tobacco products that have been chewed and discarded from other's mouths. That's plain nasty. Inmates convince their baby-mammas to hide contraband in a child's pampers. Where is the respect? Given the fact that a lot of those individuals are dealing with mental health issues, it would be unfair on my behalf not to reiterate the same. As for the rest of us, no excuse.

The lack of mental health institutions within the FBOP serve to make matters worse. The strange, and often dangerous behavior from these inmates is never properly addressed. Each action is met with punishment, while the true issue continues to fester. I can tell you to pull your pants up, mind your tongue, read your book, work out and eat your veggies, but without the ability to comprehend right from wrong, the message with be forever lost. There are over a million books on self-improvement, and thousands of inmates who can't read. Change comes from within, but first you must want change, and unfortunately a lot of inmates don't.

I sat down with old dragons and new guerrillas to discuss the conditions of today's prison system. There seems to be a clear distinction between the men who strive for betterment, and those who are socially suicidal. I asked the convicts how can the dumb, deaf and blind learn to listen, see and correct the flaws in their own actions?

"They can't!" was the most familiar answer.

At the time, my inclination was to allow others to crash. Bumps and bruises are aggressive tutors; and the pain I have suffered is enough for a driven mind to heed. That's why I don't skip, jive or fraternize with the opposition. You see, serious times call for serious minds; and silence is a lethal weapon made to be used not abused. Prisoners are sentenced to serve time. However, if we allow the time to serve us, that's how we all win as a people, as well as a nation. Our prison system encourages the incarcerated to become decrepit. On the contrary, if prisoners become decorous, and full of esteem, that's when we will achieve true power. And with power comes respect. That's why I encourage principles that bring coherence and greatness to a free society such as: personal responsibility, hard work, individual initiative, delayed gratification, commitment to excellence, competition by merit and the honor in achievement.

I was once told; the ink of a scholar is more precious than the blood of a martyr. It is what you do that will define you. Therefore, if you cannot control your sexual urges, and continue to pull out your private parts in hopes of being noticed, then you are a "Gunner". If you continue to use drugs excessively, and against your own better judgement, then you are a "Addict". And if you gather information from others, then use said information (whether true or false) to benefit yourself in other ways, you are a "snitch".

"There is no better tool in the jungle of survival than being able to identify who you are dealing with".

-Robert Greene

Likewise, if you stand on your word, say what you mean, maintain values and principles, address issues head on, protect your loved ones, talk less-do more, want for others what you want for yourself, give respect and demand the same from others, respect women, set goals and strive for the betterment of your community and just happen to be currently incarcerated, then you are a convict. And the Administration would like to eradicate your existence. They flood your community (prison compounds) with drugs and misinformation to make you more like inmates. Why? Because inmates are easier to control. Inmates put themselves before all others and depend on the Administration to provide them with purpose. Convicts don't need television, email, mp3, extra food, microwaves or any other so-called privileges that will be later used against them. Convicts only need comrade to stand with and stand on constitutional issues that our forefathers guaranteed for every American citizen. Incarcerated or not.

A lack of self-discipline on our own behalf has allowed this oppressive behavior from prison officials to become the new normal within the FBOP, our country's largest detention system. These actions are perpetuated with no real resistance from the incarcerated, due to feelings of low-self-esteem, depression and stress.

Question: "If it is as bad as you say it is, why do prisoners seem so content?"

Answer: "He loves the devil because the devil gives him nothing."

When I was sentenced to 27 years in Federal Prison, for a none-violent, victimless crime, I stood before the judge emotionless. Even though I knew I did not deserve the time I received, I did not shout, scream or complain. In a stupor, I stood there thinking about what my life had become. Then for some unknown reason to myself at the time, when the judge moved to make his ruling final, I lifted my head and said: "thank you!" WTF?

I thanked him for unjustly stealing away my youth. I thanked him for giving me more time then convicted murderers receive. Jewish men in concentration camps performed social entertainment for their captors. Prisoners complain on grievance forms then hold silent when regional directors visit the prison. Inmates joke with unit officers and smile at the warden with no hint of indignation for unfair treatment. Insanity! Or maybe not.

Studies have shown that mentally abused victims often become passive and unsure of themselves. Victims of physical abuse bottle up aggression that often explodes over small issues later. The common word here is "victims". Somewhere in the minds of the abused remains a piece of hope that their abuser might one day show some compassion. It's a long shot, but for the defeated, having a shot at all is often the only thing that wakes them up in the morning.

Prisoners of the past, such as Nelson Mandela, Malcom X, George Lester Jackson, Ben Chavis and even Michael G. Santos have written about the cruelties within the prison system. And the struggle to stop prison officials from abusing their authority continues today. This fight is not solely a race issue, it is a human issue that requires insight and oversight, strength and courage, compassion and understanding for all people. Its serious business. So then, where is the indignation from prisoners? No one can force you to talk, walk, work or smile. These are actions you, and you alone control. Even the Chinese resorted to a hundred-year silence in order to strengthen their country without influences from the outside. One hundred years! Many passive men can ignore or disregard the target of their affection when feeling shunned or dismissed. What of the prisoner? Has the feeling of past disappointments scorned so deep that we have given up on being treated fairly? Or is it the medication and drugs that keep us in front of the flat screens, while others put their public image, time and money up for a cause that will benefit us all. At the lowest level of defense, regarding our own God given right to be treated equally, a nonviolent and peaceful response would be to close your mouth and do the time. But many inmates cannot seem to do that much. Makes me wonder.

Do you know your rights? You have the right to remain silent, anything you say can and will be used against you in a court of law, you have a right to an attorney, if you cannot afford one, an attorney will be provided for you. Sound familiar?

It's a new day and prisoners must re-think and refrain from such folly as; slot jacking and overreacting to light situations that will soon work themselves out. Childish actions only add to the disrespect and help to re-enforce the programmed minds set to despise the prison population. Officers are well trained in dealing with disgruntled inmates, threatening to harm themselves through food strikes and self-mutilation. These are ancient cries for help, and desperate attempts to pull attention towards unjust actions. "What else can we do?" I hear you. And I share your pain, but confusion is no excuse. Regardless of your complaints, frustrations, pain and suffering, the Administration has a duty to keep us breathing. (Job Security). Keep us breathing, not keep us happy. So, if they must tie us down and push a clear tube up our noses to force liquids into our systems, they will! Trust me, I have suffered unexpected nose bleeds ever since.

So don't listen to the weightlifting meatheads who think the size of their biceps indicates their strength. True strength is shown through discipline. Never mind the type that cover themselves in tattoos to announce to the world how tough they are. Real toughness is in the ability to sacrifice. Disregard the blowhards who have a thousand stories about what they're going to do, but a thin record of what they have done. Hold your tongue and let your actions speak for you. To become a leader, you must first embrace reality, and be brutally honest about the harsh facts surrounding your situation.

Holding your tray slot will only result in incident reports, and another chance for the Administration to paint you in a bad light. Threats and signs of aggression will amount to the same. But no one can force you to talk or spend your own money. Some prisoners have seen success (required outcome) by "acting out". And that's the trick. Achieving a goal by risky measures often manipulates the mind into believing the method works. But success is not a destination, it's a journey. It's a flaw in criminal thinking (Now ain't that an oxymoron) to disregard "luck" and inflate the ego instead. However, if your course of action is true, you should receive the same or similar desired result with no harm to yourself. At least more times than not. But the country recidivism rate isn't high for no reason. There are too many ex-offenders that simply do not know what else to do. So, they use the same methods, chasing that one-time victory that convinced them so long ago, that if nothing else, it's possible.

And why wouldn't they? Who has taken the time away to teach them the value of hard work and difficult principles such as: Delayed gratification? Instead, prisoners spend their time on the inside, breathing! The Administrative remedy process, complete with official forms and the "chain of command" humbuggery is a joke that normally keeps prisoners in limbo while our rights are trampled on. Clearly, I'm not a fan, but they have the right idea, which is to put your issues on paper to be documented. That way, even if big brother is silently patting little brother on the back for denying a prisoner the justice he deserves, a record of the misconduct will exist. We then must find the right organization to send it to or put it all in a book. *You get the picture*. Convicts and inmates alike must start thinking outside the box. Literally! We can't demand respect, then tap dance for favor with our palms out. Respect yourself, throw away that pampered mentality, trade in aggression for indignation and belligerence for self-control. Let your silence speak out and your actions be true. "Give me what I deserve!" Nothing more, nothing less, and that will do.

CHAPTER 10

MOVING ON

On day one, I woke in the middle of the night shivering. I pulled the covers from my body and stood up to use the bathroom. The toilet was only four feet away. An easy trek, plus return trip I thought, but my body seemed to be on another course. Each step proved harder than the last as I wiggled my limbs towards the stall. Sweat poured down my forehead as I tried to control my teeth from chattering. I placed one hand on the wall and wondered what my ailment could be. The symptoms: Both hot and cold sweats, body pains and a massive headache. At that time, nothing appealed to me more than reaching my bunk and finding some soothing rest. I found my bunk, but it would be over two weeks before I received anything remotely close to a soothing rest. The next morning, I tested positive for COVID-19. In fact, 65 inmates out of 130 tested positive on the same day.

Up until that moment in time, the Coronavirus had already infected over 24 million Americans, killing over 450,000 along with 2,100 prisoners. A month prior to my positive results, there were zero cases on the cell block I was housed in. the Administration, along with our entire country were still dealing with the global pandemic, learning new ways to prevent the spread of the deadly virus while preparing to vaccinate the American people. Fully aware of the danger, the Administration at Florence Colorado USP continued to violate the number one preventive measure, ordered throughout the country and the world abroad: social distancing.

As prisoners, during and throughout the Coronavirus pandemic, we were forced to live in 8x10 cells with other individuals. This positioning made six feet distancing from other inmates impossible. Moreover, for those truly concerned about their own safety and wellbeing, every effort to protect themselves was often foiled by a different cell mate with ignorant beliefs and intentions. Needless to say, a prisoner could sleep with his mask on and still contract covid-19 from a cellmate less concerned with the seriousness of the disease.

Case and point, on Feb 2nd, 2021, The Administration at Florence Colorado USP removed two inmates from the special housing unit and relocated them to unit EA, the unit in which I was housed. These two inmates were earlier places in the special housing unit after receiving positive covid-19 testing results. Through negligence and a mismeasurement of quarantine procedures, the staff at Florence allowed these inmates to not only return to general population pre-maturely, but also to interact and mingle with other prisoners. Conventional wisdom would ask, why not further quarantine these inmates with others on similar status? There are complete units with inmates confined to their cells 23\1 who tested positive and remained on such status to ensure the safety of others. Why take the chance of an outbreak, knowing the effect such outbreak could cause in minimal timing? Why continue to move new inmates around old, SHU inmates among general population and transferees on to non-infected units? There are 62 cells on each unit. The Administration at Florence Colorado ordered all inmates housed in unit EA to be locked down in their cells for the next three days period, the first testing revealed 65 prisoners tested positive for covid-19. The Administration then pushed for another careless move. They ordered all "positive" inmates to cell up with each other, and all "negative" prisoners to join as cellmates, or else.

The violation of social distancing protocol had already taken effect. 65 positive results turned into 85 before property was moved, and cell doors secured. On day two I struggled to sit up. My body hurt in so many ways I felt as if I was assaulted by a football team. I heard prisoners talking through the cracks in their doors. The fear of losing their lives started to mount. On day three, over 120 inmates on E-A had tested positive for Covid-19. Medical staff began making rounds. "How are you feeling?" Was the common question. No advice, no suggestions for fighting off the virus in my body, just a thumbs up and a walk through. I wanted to scream, but lacked the energy to breath properly. My sister is a nurse. I wanted her help, but the administration wouldn't allow us phone calls until the fifth day. Isolated and cut off from the world, I worried that I might never hear from my loved ones again. Then I lost my taste and smell. Using the bathroom became a traumatizing event. I decided to eat in increments rather than reach for the toilet paper regularly. The thought of bending over hurt. *That bad.* It was reported that prisoners are close to five times more likely to be infected and about three times as likely to die from Covid-19 as their non-incarcerated peers. And still the negligence from staff continued.

I listened as the head of health services laughed about returning positive test results to the incarcerated. "It's like telling a 15-year-old girl that she is pregnant." Other staff members blamed the outbreak on the inmates. "If you all were wearing your masks properly, you would have been okay." No condolences or responsibility for the direct actions that caused the entire unit to contract Covid-19. On the contrary, if the administration would not have placed infected persons among non-infected persons, or provided effective masks to protect from the spread of the virus, or cared enough about the lives of the incarcerated to not force them to live in rooms the size of a broom closet with complete strangers during a global pandemic that calls for social distancing, there wouldn't be over 2,000 prisoners dead and thousands more suffering as I myself suffered from the indifference of those hired to protect me from harm.

With the vaccination developed, packaged and ready for distribution, one might think the fear from infection would subside with the joy of hope. But each state laid out their vaccine distribution plans, with Colorado deciding to put the incarcerated at the back of the line. Colorado Governor Jared Pulis changed the State's Coronavirus vaccination plan after Republican District Attorney George Brauchler railed in a Denver paper op-ed that it was unfair for the State to inoculate someone like Nathan Dunlap, convicted of murdering four people at a Chuck E. Cheese in 1993, before his 78-year-old father. In other words, let the prisoners suffer. Even though the CDC recommended that prisoners be inoculated at the same time as the guards, even though prisoners have high rates of hypertension, heart disease and other conditions that increase the possibility of infection by Covid-19, let's leave them for last. The lack of compassion for human life can become as contagious as a virus itself. Who is the criminal: the one who took a life unjustly, or the one who unjustly allowed a life to be taken?

Often times, you can't protect people from themselves. But when you force prisoners to take showers barefooted in unsanitized showers, provide no effective masks, violate social distancing measures, push business as usual during stay-at-home orders, laugh in the face of the infected, choose to fulfill transfer orders over prisoner safety and continue to increase the chances of infection, you're liable. And I hope you can accept responsibility for your action.

It's not easy to express what has been done, unfairly and unnecessarily without feeling angry. I write objectively, with no taste or smell, knowing that life affects us all in different ways. Many lives have been lost at the hands of Covid-19. And for all those who have survived, will we ever truly move on? It's hard to see the correct path to travel down while surrounded in chaos; but as we move forward, I believe it is important to learn about others through conversation and analyzation of the circumstances that motivate behaviors. Our Country consists of many different people from very different walks of life. Albeit, still people. And this includes our prison population and the staff members hired to secure them. We are not perfect. None of us. But we don't have to be either. Taking responsibility for your own actions is only a part of our human duty. Complete accountability is realizing how your actions affect others, then taking the proper steps to promote positive change. There has been no other time in my own lifespan that I can recall when there has been so many ready to listen to the cause of injustice. There are conversations being had over inequality and cruelty and this book is my contribution to the overall topic that effects us all as a nation. Because I too am alive, and I too give a damn.

"We must accept the reality that to confine offenders behind walls without trying to change them is an expensive folly with short term benefits, winning battles while losing the war."

-Chief Justice Warren Burger

In the school of right and wrong, we all have new lessons to learn. And if we can comprehend completely, the concept of compassion along with non-violence, non-prejudice, non-judgment, patience, love, charity and generosity, we grow closer together no matter our locations. In the future, I hope that we can recognize deceptions and the traps that blind our conscious and influence our silence. It's time to take an honest look at those we incarcerate: the men and women we have turned our backs on and reevaluate the value we keep locked in a cage.

I recently watched a movie interestingly titles: *Maleficent*. I found the story entertaining, intricate and revealing. Let me explain. There were two societies living on opposite sides of the land, each one looking to the other with dismay caused by lies and the lack of understanding for the other's culture. As the story unfolded, the antagonist revealed the plot. She said: "Do you know what truly makes a great ruler? It's the ability to instill fear in your subjects, then use that fear against your enemy." Let that sink in a little longer.

The Federal Bureau of Prisons advertises its primary goal as being to protect the American public. But from who? The convicted? Is this the same convicted being released back into society after decades behind bars with no help or rehabilitation skills, while the administration promotes more punishment and less reward for the incarcerated individuals they continue to look down on? Can't be! Correctional Officers are taught to despise prisoners and follow order. Even when the orders are abusive and cruel towards the inmate. Job security and social acceptance require a quiet tongue. But why do it? What motivates them to go along? Fear! Fear is a powerful incentive. It can blind the mind from reason and force an irrational response. The fear of not being safe. The fear of having no stability. The fear of being alone. There are many who will agree to just about anything in order to escape their own fears.

People carry concealed weapons based on fear. New laws are implemented based on fear. Countries are captured and dismantled based on fear. Lives are taken prematurely based on fear. Men and women are given outrageous jail terms based on fear. But who are we afraid of? Is it your neighbor? The garbage man? Uber driver? Barber, landlord, mechanic, florist, gym instructor, mailman? Or just the prisoners? Because many ex-offenders become all of those things once released from prison. Do our fears extend to those walking among us, or are they exclusively reserved for those in khaki jumpsuits and restraints?

Conservatives will say, "Maybe we should just let them all out. End prison all together and allow dangerous thugs to harm whomever they want."

Now that's being extreme. I'm not advocating to end prisons. What I'm suggesting is that, we as a nation, no longer allow our fears to overpower our reason. I'm asking for prisoners to be treated fairly. Prisons are still very much needed and valued in any civilized society. However, who is being punished, how are they being treated and the reason for their incarceration calls for powerful voices to meet at the table and have a real discussion on reform and the future direction of our justice system.

Remember the drug dealer? That evil element living among us, waving illegal (or legal) narcotics in our faces, tempting us to escape our own reality, influencing our vices and benefitting from our lack of self-discipline. He has taken advantage of us! Now allow me to direct your attention to the other side of town.

The FBOP incarcerates the mentally ill, charges them for use of facility communication devices, solicitates funds from their family members, puts legal drugs in their systems, charges them fines for behavior they can't control, inflicts pain to force cooperation, physically assaults them, forces unwanted associations, uses fear tactics, creates drug dependencies and causes low self-esteem, all while receiving a paycheck courtesy of the American public. They're taking advantage of us! Well, aren't they?

Drugs are a problem. Not drug dealers, but drugs! Since the Civil War, American veterans have returned home with many different injuries that lead to drug use. Habits turn into addictions, and users turn to dealers. But our justice system doesn't penalize users with lengthy prison time. Why not? What happened to tough on crime? Only the drug dealer takes that hit, while users go on to become Correctional Officers. Who should be held responsible for the drug users' addiction? In the late 80's, many media outlets credited the death of NBA draft pick Len Bias as the push that sparked the "War on Drugs". The talented basketball star died from an overdose while celebrating his signing to the Boston Celtics. A user! He made a conscious choice to put cocaine in his own body to heighten his environment. A user, not a drug dealer, but a drug user. And over thirty years later, millions have been sentenced to prison for the choice that one user consciously made. I mean no disrespect to the Bias family, but we cannot correct injustice without taking responsibility for our own actions. The war on drugs is and always has been completely Bias!

At least Oregon got it right. A 2021 article reported that the State legalized all drugs in favor of treatment over prison time and money fines over convictions. It's the right thing to do. I can only hope that our country soon follows Oregon's lead. The law should be enforced equally or not at all.

Similarly so, an inmate who suffers from Post-Traumatic Stress should never be forced to pay a hundred dollar fine every time he is found to be in possession of a weapon. Where is the help? Prisoners who have shown themselves to be psychotic should never be forced to cell with violent offenders. Where is the protection? Who controls these choices, or is the "control" the only objective? Correctional officers and staff members alike need to learn "problem and resolution" skills. Too many guards are prone to creating altercations instead of resolving them. They are handed a set of keys and a uniform, ordered to report to duty and placed in a unit with no plan of operation; leaving the prisoners unsure of how to conduct themselves based on inconsistent rules and miscommunication from staff. This confusion often leads to incident reports for conduct accepted by one guard and rejected by another. What are the rules?

The Administration creates policies and then breaks them. Inmates are bullied and abused, stripped of their individualism and verbally assaulted every day of incarceration. But a prison sentence shouldn't require a human being to become less than. Prison staff members are often hired based on their lack of compassion for the incarcerated. Ex-service men are preferred based on their ability to follow orders without a conscious or rebuttal. But American prisoners are still American citizens, and if the FBOP continues to allow cruel and unfair treatment, they are not protecting the American public at all, and it only causes a worse problem in the interest of corruption.

Whatever happened to "serve and protect?" Officers used to be honored for putting their own lives in harm's way to save another. Today it is more common to see an officer take another's life in order to protect his own. They are taught to save themselves. "Staff" is placed in front of "inmate" at every turn. Even with staff members being terminated and prosecuted for illegal acts on Federal grounds, yet and still, an officer's word continues to be superior to that of the convict.

"There is no blind eye applied to prison officials' misconduct."

No, it's just swept under the rug until the mess is too great to ignore. The fact of the matter is, staff members are protected by staff members. The Administrative Remedy process is designed to protect Staff, not the prisoners. Staff members are supplied with weapons and tactics to defend themselves, while prisoners are labeled enemies in their own country. People who harm other people should be punished, including staff members. There are unchecked mental illnesses on both sides, and until we, as a country, address the real issues, we will all continue to be victimized by the indifference.

My associations should be a choice; not forced upon me. I choose not to associate with child molesters. Not because of the crimes they have committed, but because of their mentality, and the threat they continue to pose towards our nation's youth. I choose not to associate with snitches or informants. Not because of their cooperation with law enforcement, but because of their selfish nature, lack of moral code and the opportunistic train of thought that puts others in danger of losing what we should rightfully have. I choose not to befriend drug addicts. Not because of their lack of self-control, but because of their constant dependency and failure to comprehend reason is a threat to my personal property and physical health. Do I not have a right to protect myself from these elements? If so, why am I punished for doing so?

I understand that I am buried alive in the justice system and my opinion, which has been shaped by my personal experiences, will be scrutinized by many, but I have never assaulted a child, offered information to others in order to escape my own crimes, abused drugs, or use another person's addiction against them. I graduated from the School of Hard Knocks and enrolled into the University of Adversity. I gained a Bachelor's Degree from a State Pen and my Master's Degree from a USP. I'm different, and I have a right to be. My hands are not clean, but I know wrong from right. There are many prisoners who need help, not punishment. And until they receive it, I will always protect myself, my family, my personal thoughts and property from any threats, as the constitution clearly allows.

How many of you would allow a mentally or criminally insane person to sleep above or below you? "That's part of the punishment," one might say. My answer: Then the punishment is not only cruel, but the psychological effects on a prisoner will soon unfairly victimize others. Hurt people, hurt people. Why is it acceptable to neglect the incarcerated? I offer this:

The Dark Knight is another quality film I once saw. Everyone loved to hate the Joker. There is a scene in the film when he sits bedside with a badly injured prosecutor and explains the "normal order of things." In a nutshell, there is no outcry for the mistreatment or death of a prisoner, because he is a prisoner. Prisoners die, they fight, get stabbed, serve a lot of time, complain about things and act out. It's acceptable (normal order of things). Even our Country's media outlets felt it irrelevant to waste time and ink on the 2,000 deaths of prisoners at numerous institutions due to the Coronavirus outbreaks. In the eyes of many, prisoners were already infected way before the Coronavirus arrives. They are scum. Who cares about that?

Over half a million lives were lost in our country during the Covid-19 pandemic. That's more deaths than World War II, that our country will be forced to remember for many years to come. What I will remember is the late reaction by prison staff members, the lack of concern, prisoner's family members passing away without being able to say goodbye, officers coughing in the open air and laughing at the clear threat they posed to others, being forced into special housing units to lessen my family communication, being forced to accept a cellmate until the entire unit became infected with Covid-19, my life placed in jeopardy for no true reason and the pain that covered my body as it fought to survive. During a national crisis, the FBOP neglected the prisoners they were ordered to protect. Lompoc became one of the worst facilities in dealing with the outbreak, with over 900 inmates infected at one time. Their practice of not providing prisoners with proper cleaning supplies no doubt added to their negligence. Overall, it's the FBOP's strategy to terrorize the inmate population, instead of sympathize, that puts every convicted man or woman in harm's way, every day of incarceration, virus or no virus.

What now? The Bureau of Prisons should contact the family members of every inmate who lost his or her life due to complications from Coronavirus and offer compensation for the invaluable lives that are no longer with us. They should use every dollar taken from prisoners though unjust fines within the system, overpriced commissary items, inmate trust funds and all bonuses given to Wardens at the end of the physical year for scaling back spending and shortening the prison population on what they have coming, and donate it all to the families of the prisoners victimized by the Coronavirus and the indifference on behalf of the prison staff. They should stop penalizing the mentally ill and those suffering from depression. They should stop forcing prisoners to take responsibility for other prisoner's actions, and train staff members to not abuse their authority. They should eradicate trouble causing Wardens who punish the prison population in order to stir up problems, and promote family ties along with new positive friendships with law-abiding citizens.

Prison officials should help the convicted become better people, guide them in the right direction, and refrain from punishing with no cause. Reward good conduct and outstanding achievements. Remind prisoners that they are people too, and one step in the right direction is a start towards progression. True freedom is not about being able to do whatever you like, rather being able to do what you truly want in spite of what others may think. Correctional officers have to find the courage to do what is right, not socially acceptable, regardless of their fears. And America needs to face its drug use problem and start taking responsibility for the part we all play in the illegal sale of narcotics. Yeah, I said it.

Although I have been personally victimized by our justice system, I understand that it is very difficult to help those that won't help themselves. Prisoners, inmates, convicts and ex-offenders, we have to do better. Period! Success requires no explanation and failure permits none. There were many incarcerated men who were released early due to the Coronavirus pandemic. Some never made it to their homes, while others were blessed to reunite with their loved ones. Unfortunately, some of these men returned to jail with new charges shortly after being released. I understand more than most the pressure of suddenly returning to society with no plans, education or job skills. The feeling of responsibility alone can overwhelm. But we must do better. There are conversations being had, lines being pushed and people standing up for a cause not their own. We must do our part. I can't stress this point enough.

I am a man before anything else. Titles do not define me. I am an individual, and according to the Constitution I have a right to be. I hold morals and principles I wish to protect from infectious behaviors and the manipulation of others. In my pursuit of happiness, I have a right to be safe from harm, both physically and mentally. If those who are hired to ensure my protection shall fail or neglect their duties, I will take up the proper measures to secure my own survival. It's the American way.

Vivek Murphy was the 19th Surgeon General of the United States. During the Coronavirus pandemic, he published a book titled: *Loneliness*. In it, he spoke vividly about the healing power of human connection and how the American people will survive tragedy and start anew by building together. I like that: "Building together." Consider the millions who were ordered to stay inside and practice social distancing throughout the many waves of Covid-19. Anger and frustration, mixed with loneliness and anxiety. Many simply couldn't take it. Some broke out of their homes seeking some form of entertainment that resembled their "normal" lives. Why? Because people need that healthy human physical connection that fills the spirit. Vivek Murphy was right, but like so many others around the nation, he forgot to add the prisoners in the overall conversation.

The prisoners who have been locked down and without physical contact visits for over a year now. The prisoners, cut off from the world in ways that have left us craving for information. I woke up and found out that we lost the Black Mamba and the Black Panther in the same year. I felt like Ant Man, shocked to see a field of names long gone as my mind tried to catch up.

I may have survived the Coronavirus, but new strains continue to threaten the unvaccinated. In a year that televised civil unrest and scandalous plots to overturn a free election, what about the prisoners? Do we even matter?

"When you see something that is not right, nor fair, not just, it is my philosophy that you have a moral obligation to get in trouble, to make some noise, and to point people in a different direction."

-Rep. John Lewis

So, I might spend the next ten summers in solitary confinement for taking up an issue many consider trivial, but I refuse to sit by while the prison administration continues to program its workers to disassemble prisoners' sense of self-worth, confidence, masculinity, dignity and overall health by dehumanizing tactics designed to belittle and humiliate. How many books must be written on mass incarceration, the new Jim Crow or the effect of an unjust system? Is business as usual simply too profitable to even consider a new direction? Where are the mental institutions and substance abuse programs in the conversation of reform? Is the physical and mental abuse of prisoners truly a part of the punishment? If so, what does that say about us as a nation? Should drug dealers continue to take full responsibility for America's drug addiction? And what about the user? Are we too ashamed to raise a hand and take equal weight for our own actions? Will the snitch continue to be allowed to commit crimes with immunity? Will criminal ties and associations continue to be forced on inmates and prisoners alike? Is the death of over 2,000 prisoners not worth of media attention?

The Coronavirus opened our eyes to the true value of the life we live and the uncertainty that tomorrow provides. In doing so, I hope it also opened our ears so that we can now gain a better understanding about the importance of treating each other fairly. There is still so much to do. A conversation is merely a bridge that can connect two worlds. I'm a prisoner. They won't listen to me, but they just might listen to us. Let's talk about it.

Continue the conversation.

"We cannot improve what we're not willing to measure."

-The We Must Count Coalition.

By B. A., Charles Irving Ellis

AFTERWARDS

As the COVID-19 global pandemic continued to spread across the world, it later produced new variants of the virus such as the Delta virus and the Omicron virus, pushing the death toll past six million globally, including over one million Americans and 2,000 American prisoners. Residual symptoms such as fatigue, shortness of breath, sleeping disorders, fevers, gastrointestinal issues, anxiety, depression, and brain fog helped create terms like Long COVID.

Myself, along with the entire prison population at USP Florence, were offered vaccination with no penalties applied for those that denied treatment. Unfortunately, prison staff members were not rewarded with such volition. BOP officials ordered all guards to achieve full vaccination by November 22, 2021 (later moving the date) or face termination. A gutsy call by an administration attempting to demonstrate its humanity and concern for the future health of the prisoners they were hired to protect. And although 90 percent of the prisoners had already contracted the deadly virus, the push for staff vaccination appeared to be a diligent one. It wasn't.

I was once told that, given the chance, most people will show you exactly who they are and how they feel about you. The government's ultimatum was met with resistance and petition by large numbers of correctional officers. Picket signs arrived in front of the institution, held by employees refusing to be pushed around. I'm sure they had their reasons. Many American citizens struggled with the choice of being vaccinated or ostracized. Freedom for all! That is, unless that freedom affects the bottom line. The government's vain attempt to make the prison safer during the pandemic only served the opposite. Less guards reported to work as more news cameras covered the fallout. Less guards equaled less security. Prisoner movement was restricted. Programming canceled. Family communication was cut off while prisoners received punishment for the infractions of others. It was only a matter of time before something more tragic hit.

The FBOP is reactive, never proactive. They hustle to contain problems only after said problem has affected others. They have no real interest in preventing problems from happening in the first place. Why? While staff clashed over the issue of vaccination, the shortage of guards failed to prevent three murders (inmate stabbings) within three months' time. Three prisoners lost their lives unnecessarily, and an indefinite lockdown ensued. Prisoners understand that they will be punished for the actions of others, but does that make it right? Let's take a look at what one of the top global thinkers and author of "David and Goliath" Malcolm Gladwell has to say:

"When people in authority want the rest of us to behave, it matters first and foremost how they behave. This is called the 'principle of legitimacy,' and legitimacy is based on three things: first of all, the people who are asked to obey authority have to feel like they have a voice; second, the law has to be predictable; there has to be a reasonable expectation that the rules tomorrow are going to be roughly the same as the rules today. And third, the authority has to be fair.

"All good parents understand these three principles implicitly. If you want to stop lil Johnnie from hitting his sister, you can't look away one time and scream at him another. How you punish is as important as the act of punishing itself."

Is he right? Why were we not locked down indefinitely after the first murder? Why is it that each new guard working a unit is left to decide on which policies to follow and which ones to ignore? Who wrote these policies, and why does the prisoner have no say in the fairness of each "rule" said to be in place to protect his or her own life? There is no consistency. There is no fairness. There is no concern, and that's why such authority is illegitimate. All prisoners are punished for the actions of one prisoner. All prisoners lose the privileges they have earned for the actions of the ones that don't care. Meanwhile, no guards are penalized for the actions of their coworkers. Are they that holy and beyond reproach? I argue not.

A former guard employed by the Federal Burau of Prisons at the Correctional Institute in Aliceville, Alabama was sentenced on October 26, 2021, to an 18-month prison term followed by five years of supervised release. According to a statement by the federal Department of Justice, the guard, 32-year-old Eric Todd Ellis, pleaded guilty to one count of sexually abusing a ward for having sex with a BOP prisoner in the prison laundry room on June 11, 2020.

In April 2019, a former chaplain at the Federal Correctional Institution in Berlin, Joseph Buenviaje, was sentenced to 40 months in federal prison for bringing suboxone, synthetic cannabinoids, marijuana, tobacco, and cell phones into the prison, selling enough to earn $52,000 in bribes from prisoners he was supposed to be ministering to.

In December 2019, former BOP prison guard Paul Anton Wright pleaded guilty to accepting bribes to smuggle tobacco, synthetic marijuana, and suboxone into FCI Fort Dix. He was also ordered to surrender $50,000 he had earned in the 2015 scheme, which prosecutors said he used to support a gambling habit at Atlantic City casinos.

Also in New York City, September 2020, BOP guard Robert Adams pleaded guilty to accepting sex from a prisoner's visitor in exchange for allowing her to bring contraband into Metropolitan Correctional Center—the same lockup where billionaire accused child sex trafficker Jeffrey Epstein committed suicide in 2019 while guards were sleeping and browsing the internet.

In March 2021, another federal judge handed down a 46-month sentence to a former guard at FCI Texarkana, James Thompson, after he pleaded guilty to smuggling cell phones, tobacco, and other substances to prisoner Gilbert Gomez.

In September 2019, a judge sentenced two former guards at Jessup Correctional Institution who were convicted of smuggling contraband to prisoners in the Crips gang, which was led by one of the guards, Antoine Fordham. He received a 35-year prison term with no more than 15 years suspended. The other former guard, Phillipe Jordan, was given a 10-year sentence.

In December 2020, guard Billie Michelle Hester was arrested for allegedly selling cell phones at $250 a pop to prisoners under her watch at the Walker County Jail in Jasper, Alabama.

In August 2020, just a year and a day after he was hired as a guard at the W.C. "Dub" Brassell Detention Center in Arkansas, Corey Hayes was arrested and charged with attempting to bring marijuana, rolling papers, tobacco, and cell phones into the jail.

Are correctional officers forced to suffer for the actions of their coworkers? Have guards been restricted from becoming chaplains or banned from carrying electric devices to work? Has the administration even taken a serious look at the cause and effect of unfair treatment? I think not. Prison should be about rehabilitation rather than retribution. Rehabilitation, even for those you do not like.

Pulitzer Prize winner Jared Diamond wrote that, "The remaining purpose behind punishing convicted criminals is to rehabilitate them so that they can re-enter society, resume a normal life and make an economic contribution to society instead of imposing a heavy economic cost on society as prisoners of our costly prison system."

I agree, but when does rehabilitation start? Can one learn to follow the rules while they are applied unequally? How can you see me (a prisoner) clearly when the facts are twisted in order to present a false reflection? E.g. the prisoner Individualized Needs Plan program review displays: pending charges, detainers, current work assignments, current education information, discipline history, current care assignment, current drug assignments, long-term goals and FSA assignments, all written, chosen, and decided by staff members without speaking to the prisoner or conducting an interview. What this "program review" does not mention nor recognize is the productive goals I have achieved such as: read over 500 books, learned a second language, published numerous books, graduated from career school, maintained strong family ties, all while jumping the hurdles of being dyslexic. Why do they hide the positive and flaunt the negative? Who decided to label me "high risk recidivism" when the fact is I haven't committed a crime since my 22nd birthday (over 20 years ago); I am a graduate with strong family support, including a NAACP president (my mother), an attorney (my sister), a registered nurse (my sister), and a licensed accountant (my father). Even my sentencing judge noted that I have more potential than most defendants. This was stated right before he handed me a 27-year prison sentence for a nonviolent, victimless crime. Some potential.

Our justice system continues to produce misleading information, while career felons are paid with government tax money and allowed to remain on the streets. In the same year that we lost countless lives, the government handed out millions of dollars to informants (snitches) that helped secure wrongful convictions. Some prisoners were released on court motions during the pandemic, only to be ordered back to prison before the coronavirus conclusion. To quote the great Nelson Mandela fully: "It is said that no one truly knows a nation until one has been inside its jails. A nation should not be judged by how it treats its highest citizen, but its lowest ones."

Question: How are the prisoners treated?

Answer: With indifference.

The psychological side effects of oppression often go unnoticed, unrecognized, and untreated. In prison it's about perception. The Bureau doesn't see human beings with mental issues that need help. They only see inmates who committed crimes and deserve punishment. Meanwhile, prisoners have lost hope in a system designed to destroy their sense of self-worth and individualism. The administration carries out mandates that leave the incarcerated feeling worthless and without hope while denying them the true joys of life.

Social suicide is a moral and also ethical submission to the disdainful opinions of others: You think I ain't shit, therefore, I ain't shit. Prisoners continue to disfigure their faces, distort their minds, and mentally separate themselves from a world they feel will never accept them. Self-mutilation becomes a symbolic F-bomb to the oppressor. For the incarcerated, our appearance is often the only thing we control.

Correction officers offer restraints but no corrections. They use tactics of abuse to maintain order but never present new methods of thinking for those with twisted mentalities. Too often as a society do we stare at the effect and ignore the cause. When condemning the "monster" without ever addressing the "maker." Correctional guards are enabled by the administration to maintain a system of abuse. They are encouraged to never trust the convicted, follow orders, and always "appear" firm and fair. The FBOP is reactive, never proactive. Hence, their response to the coronavirus outbreak. What's the excuse? You didn't know that exposing the prisoner population to incoming transfers would increase the chances of spreading the virus? Maybe you missed the nationwide social distancing orders blasted all over news stations. Or is it that the administration is not interested in preventing cruel and unusual acts aimed at the inmates they house? Only after we were all infected by negligence did talk of solutions come about. And this is the system that the America public pay to support.

In one year, the federal system executed more men and women than the entire 20 years prior. These executions were carried out during the same year that the coronavirus claimed over 500,000 American lives. Same year in which the American public said goodbye to dozens of past stars and global heroes. Has life itself lost value?

Questions over the safety of prisoners continue to go unanswered as family members worry about the lockdowns and the effects of the viruses, past and present. These issues cause depression for the incarcerated as we question the value of our own existence.

What more is there to say about a system that won't even consider releasing nonviolent offenders during a pandemic, knowing that the overpopulation of prisoners will surely increase the chances of death, while prosecutors promote get-out-of-jail-free cards for those willing to help incarcerate others? Good conduct often equals more punishment by way of circumstance within a system that penalizes all for the actions of one. The reality of this psychological warfare is that it subsequently affects us all. Consequently, the prisoner is made to suffer in silence. Even a sane mind would soon yield to the pressure of isolated turmoil. With death around the corner, we are cut off from the world and not allowed to empathize with those who have lost. Relationships are destroyed. Communication blocked. Yet we are asked to maintain. Why? So that the inmate population can resume a life of exploitation and embezzlement through unfair work wages.

The "Trust Fund" account is one giant account managed by BOP staff where federal prisoners can store their money to purchase commissary items, phone and email minutes, and send funds to family or book sellers to have books delivered. However, these accounts are not the normal bank accounts and are not subject to the same scrutiny as what the general public might face with their personal accounts. Instead, law enforcement agencies say that there's a risk of abuse, money laundering, and corruption because of the lack of oversight of these Trust Fund accounts.

As a whole, the BOP Trust fund account totals more than $100 million. This is according to the Washington Post, which cites an anonymous source within the BOP. It is not illegal for prisoners to have large sums of money in their accounts. Sometimes the sale of property or cashing out retirement accounts wind up in a prisoner's Trust Fund account simply because there's no other place to put it. Not all prisoners are fortunate enough to have an account at a regular bank where their money can earn interest for them. Instead, they are left with the BOP's non-interest-bearing Trust Fund account which earns interest for the BOP. That's right, $100 million bearing interest for the administration yearly. Not their money, but ours.

Meanwhile, prisoners are paid cents on the dollar while the money on the Trust Fund accounts earns more monthly than they do yearly. Where does this money go? Why does staff receive financial bonuses while prisoners are robbed of their personal property and rightful wages? The First Step Act (FSA) was supposed to change things. Instead, it's business as usual. Prisoners like myself remain thousands of miles away from our homes, programming is stalled or altered to delay justice from manifesting. Here at Florence USP, staff continue to claim that only "eligible" prisoners are eligible for eligible FSA 2018 programming. This play on words is intentional. Only staff members decide who is "eligible" while rewriting the law to fit their own agenda. On January 15, 2022, the USA Today newspaper printed an article that stated: "The justice department will begin transferring thousands of inmates out of federal prisons this week as part of a sweeping criminal justice overhaul, signed by President Donald Trump more than three years ago. Under the law signed in December 2018, inmates are eligible to earn time credit—10 days to 15 days of credit for every 30 days they participate in prison programs to reduce recidivism. The announcement of a finalized rule being published comes about two months after the department's inspector general sounded an alarm that the Bureau of Prisons had not applied the earned time credits to about 60,000 federal inmates who had completed the programs. It also comes a week after an announcement that the director of the prison agency, Michael Carvajal, will resign from his position in the face of mounting criticism over his leadership."

The FSA 2018 doesn't say that "eligible" inmates will receive time cuts for programming. It clearly states that, "Inmates are eligible to earn." So then, what's the hold up? Job security and social acceptance. There are powers in play that do not want to see prisoners released early; even the "eligible" ones. In prison, conflict is welcomed so that tougher policies can be created. Labels are placed on prisoners without proper screening or true justification. Faces become numbers as policies are written to punish. Am I overreacting, or has my close examination brought us closer to a squeaky door labeled Criminal Justice? Prisoners need rehabilitation, not retribution. Society needs the rehabilitated, not the angry and vengeful.

I had a conversation the other day with a guard. He told me that he believes prison should be much harder. I asked him why and he explained that the conditions impact the recidivism. Understanding that he had never served time on the inside, I attempted to explain the long-term effects of unjust punishment. He listened, and in doing so, he heard where I was coming from. "Your past is not your future. Why should one continue to pay for what has already been done?" #convictconversation

"In any dangerous environment, accumulated experience teaches rules of behavior to minimize the risks, rules worth following even if an outsider considers it overreacting." – Jared Diamond

I decided to write this book for many reasons. There are so many without a voice. While in prison it's easy to be overlooked or forgotten. For those without the words to express what they are feeling, for the illiterate, searching for a way to communicate with the world. My intentions are honest, and without a proper grievance system, my concerns continue to fall on deaf ears. There are many who refuse to believe such evil lives here in today's world. We study history and shun the tactics that helped build our nation while maintaining similar moves to keep it. Prisons are needed. I'm not here to debate that. However, it matters how we punish and how prisoners are treated. My goal is to shed light on the "makers" so that the "monsters" can be understood and handled properly.

I stand on my words. The criminal justice system cannot be fixed from the outside alone. There needs to be conversations and dialect that includes the prisoner. A seat at the table. Otherwise, the administration manual on how to make institutions safer and save lives will continue to exist with missing chapters and false pretenses. I am a prisoner. I'm also an artist, an author, an athlete, and an activist. It's easy to condemn that which you don't understand. Some are convicted off intentions alone. If my convictions show my intentions, I believe that I'm not the only one seeking a fair system. Change is inevitable, and unlike the past, we all have the opportunity to affect tomorrow. We the People. In freedom or debt. I work towards a better day and hope that you don't judge me too harshly for that...the conversation continues at Twitter@convictconversation.

I Am More

I am more than the situation I face
Beyond skin and bones, I remain unseen
I am more than my physical physique
I am deep beyond measure, I am equal and free
I'm often told to uphold and subtract what is me
To reform in the form of those more passive and weak
But I am massive, I even beat disaster,
I see far beyond procrastination's attraction to me
I strive to succeed and breed a better me
I eat difficult for breakfast, impossible shall be a feast
I treat sorrow with the truth, it soothes my distress
I tell less to bring me more until more brings me rest
I am more than a man both confined and suppressed
I am more than I am for I am blessed by the best.

CPSIA information can be obtained
at www.ICGtesting.com
Printed in the USA
LVHW080524101222
734929LV00013B/566

9 781637 510896